A DAY

AT THE

RACES

BOOKS BY BARRY GIFFORD

NON-FICTION

A Day at the Races
The Devil Thumbs a Ride & Other Unforgettable Films
The Neighborhood of Baseball
Saroyan: A Biography (with Lawrence Lee)
Jack's Book: An Oral Biography of Jack Kerouac (with Lawrence Lee)

FICTION

A Good Man to Know
An Unfortunate Woman
Port Tropique
Francis Goes to the Seashore
Landscape with Traveler: The Pillow Book of Francis Reeves
A Boy's Novel

POETRY

Ghosts No Horse Can Carry: Collected Poems
Giotto's Circle
Beautiful Phantoms: Selected Poems
Persimmons: Poems for Paintings
The Boy You Have Always Loved
Selected Poems of Francis Jammes (translations, with Bettina Dickie)
Coyote Tantras
The Blood of the Parade

BARRY GIFFORD

A DAY

AT THE

RACES

The Education of a Racetracker

THE ATLANTIC MONTHLY PRESS   NEW YORK

Portions of this book have appeared, mostly in a different form,
in the San Francisco *Chronicle* and *Rolling Stock*.

The names of certain persons in this book have been changed at
their request.

Published simultaneously in Canada
Printed in the United States of America
First Edition
Library of Congress Cataloging-in-Publication Data
Gifford, Barry, 1946-
    A day at the races.
    1. Horse-racing. 2. Horse-racing—United States.
I. Title
SF334.G5 1988   798.4'00973   87-19526
ISBN 0-87113-195-1

Designed by Julie Duquet
Illustrations by Jose Ortega

The Atlantic Monthly Press
19 Union Square West
New York, NY 10003

First printing

THIS BOOK IS FOR SUNNY DAY AWAY

ACKNOWLEDGMENTS

Most prominent among those whose assistance proved invaluable during the research and writing of this book were Richard Somers, Lafe Bassett and Floyd Prospero. Their knowledge of the various aspects of modern-day horse racing and their willingness to share their expertise with me is deeply appreciated. Others who helped in significant ways were Michael Wolfe, Art Lobato, Ellis Davis, Steve Friedman, Art Robinson, John Bryant, Vinnie Deserio, Ann Godoff and Peter Ginsberg. Thanks also to Vic Holchak, Steve Fagin, Joe Tharp, Swifty Swift, Donald S. Ellis, Tony Noll and Father Dan Noll.

Research for this book was done at Golden Gate Fields, Belmont Park, Churchill Downs, Hialeah, Longchamp, Turf Paradise and Del Mar racetracks.

Hwilum heaporofe hleapan leton
on geflit faran felawe mearas,
õaer him foldwegas faegere puhton
cystum cuõe . . .
Hwilum flutende fealwe straete
mearum maeton.

From time to time the renowned
warriors let their bay horses
gallop,—run on in races, where
the country tracks seemed suitable,—
excellent in repute . . .
Once again they covered the
straight roads strewn with sand,
racing with their horses.

—Beowulf

AUTHOR'S NOTE

This book is a portrait of Thoroughbred horse racing as it exists in the present time on any particular day at any track in the United States. It is not intended as a complete history of the game; for that, I refer the interested reader to *The History of Horse Racing* by Roger Longrigg and *The Complete Book of Thoroughbred Horse Racing* by Tom Biracree and Wendy Insinger. Neither is it a fictional or casually anecdotal treatment of the subject, the finest examples of which can be found in *Of Horses and Men: An Anthology of Horse-Racing Stories,* edited by W. George Isaak. The individuals described and who speak in these pages possess a knowledge and love of horse racing deserving of attention by anyone interested in the subject for any reason and from any angle. A day at the races is full of surprises: of fear, anger, sadness, betrayal, elation, failure and success—all wrapped up in the approximately one-half turn of the earth around the sun it takes to encompass the first predawn workouts to the finish of the last race. This is the way it looks, feels, sounds and what it means to a racetracker today.   —B.G.

CONTENTS

Cast of Characters

Locations of North Ame

MAP KEYS

1 Ak-Sar-Ben
2 Albuquerque
3 Aqueduct
4 Arlington Park
5 Assiniboia Downs
6 Atlantic City
7 Atokad Park
8 Balmoral
9 Bay Meadows
10 Belmont
11 Beulah Park
12 Birmingham Turf Club
13 Blue Ribbon Downs
14 Boise (Les Bois)
15 Calder Race Course
16 Caliente
17 Canterbury Downs
18 Charles Town
19 Churchill Downs
20 Columbus
21 Delaware Park
22 Del Mar
23 Delta Downs
24 Detroit Race Course
25 James C. Ellis Park
26 El Comandante
27 Erie Downs
28 Evangeline Downs
29 Exhibition Park
30 Fair Grounds
31 Fairmount Park
32 Fairplex Park
33 Ferndale
34 Finger Lakes
35 Fonner Park
36 Fort Erie
37 Fresno
38 Garden State Park
39 Golden Gate Fields
40 Grants Pass
41 Great Falls
42 Greenwood
43 Gulfstream Park
44 Harbor Park
45 Hawthorne
46 Hialeah Park
47 Hipodromo de las Americas
48 Hollywood Park
49 Jefferson Downs
50 Keeneland

an Thoroughbred Tracks

PROLOGUE

I

In the time of King Timaeus, briefly before 1500 B.C., Egypt was invaded from the East by a tribe named the Hyksos. Called "Shepherd Kings" or "Captive Shepherds," the Hyksos were ruled at that time by Salatis; he made all Egypt tributary, establishing military outposts throughout the country. Salatis and his successors ruled Egypt for more than five hundred years, the first two hundred of which were spent in a furious effort to eradicate completely the indigenous people. The Hyksos are believed by some to have been Arabs; others identify them with the Israelites.

Following a rebellion at Thebes in approximately 1000 B.C., the Shepherd Kings were rounded up by the Egyptian commander Misphragmuthosis and barricaded in Avaris. Misphragmuthosis's son, Thutmosis, subsequently failed in his attempt to conquer the Hyksos entirely, and finally allowed them to leave Egypt. The Shepherd Kings, a quarter-million of them, resettled in Judea and established the city of Jerusalem.

According to the book of Manetho, the first six Hyksos monarchs—Salatis, Beon, Apachnas, Apophis, Jannas and Asses—were called the "six foreign Phoenecians." In 1847, the historian E. de Rougé proved from a papyrus obtained by the British Museum that the last Hyksos king was Apopi, a ruler who replaced the worship of the Egyptian gods with his own god, named Setekh or Seti. Statuary discovered in 1861 by Mariette at Tanis had various "un-Egyptian" features, and one of these had the name Apopi engraved on it. It was at that time concluded that the features of the statues were those of the Hyksos.

The headless statue of a king named Khyan, unearthed at Bubastis about the same time, was believed to belong to the Hyksos. Khyan's name was later discovered on a statue of a lion found in Baghdad. Flinders Petrie then isolated a group of kings whose names, including Khyan's, were emblazoned on scarabs of a particular type. Archaeologists decided that these gems, cut in the forms of beetles, belonged to the Hyksos, whose appellation now became recognizable as Hek-hos, "ruler of the barbarians," a title conferred upon Khyan.

It was the Hyksos who brought to Eastern Europe and North Africa the horse. This descendant of Eohippus, the "dawn horse" of fifty million years ago, was a different breed altogether than the hirsute and stocky equine found farther north and among the Mongol tribes. It is the descendant of the horses transported to Egypt and the Eastern Mediterranean by the Hyksos that are the racehorses of today, the Thoroughbreds. *All* Thoroughbreds are descended from three stallions: The Byerly Turk, The Godolphin Arabian and The Darley Arabian, whose son, Bulle Rock, was the first Thoroughbred to go to America.

It was my mother who introduced me to horse racing. She loved going to the track and often took me with her when I was a little boy. In Florida, at Hialeah, I loved to watch the pink flamingos pick their way among the fluttering green and yellow palms; and in Chicago, at Arlington Park or Sportsman's or Maywood, I loved to listen to the heavyset, well-dressed men with diamond pinkie rings and ruler-length Havana cigars as they fussed over my mother, asking if she'd like something to eat or drink or if she wanted them to place a bet for her.

My father rarely, if ever, went to the racetrack. There may have been a bookmaking operation in the basement of his liquor store, but he told me that he didn't bet on anything with more than two legs that couldn't speak English. I doubt seriously if he'd ever heard of Xanthos, one of the two immortal horses of Achilles (the other being Balius), who had the power of speech and prophesied his master's death. If he had, I'm certain it would have served only to disaffect him further.

When I was in high school I became a real devotee of the so-called sport of kings. My friend Big Steve and I would often head for the track as soon as classes let out. Big Steve was a canny and gutsy bettor who won more often than he lost. Such was not the same in my case. I had as many off days as on, and I always felt fortunate when I broke even. But there came a day I knew I couldn't lose. I was sixteen and Gun Bow, with Walter Blum up, was running in the feature race at A.P. I was certain there were no other horses in the eighth race that day that could beat Gun Bow, who was destined to be named Horse of the Year, beating out the great Kelso, a four-time winner of the award. The one problem for me was that I was broke at the time, so I had to borrow what I could in order to bet.

Big Steve was generous and loaned me twenty bucks. He was going through one of his periodic phases of gambling abstinence. Steve decided that he'd been gambling too much of late — horses, cards, craps — and he would test his willpower by refusing to bet on Gun Bow, even though he agreed with me that it was as close to a sure thing as there could possibly be. He even offered to drive me to the track and stand by me during the race.

Now, there are sure things and there are *sure* things. Gun Bow belonged in the former category. An example of the latter was the time my friend D.A. and I stopped before the first race to visit his uncle, Ralphie Love, who was working one of the ten-dollar combination windows in the clubhouse. Ralphie was a self-described "semi-retired businessman" who had formerly been in the vending-machine business. He now worked part-time at the track and spent a lot of time attending sports events. I used to see him regularly at college basketball games in Chicago in the early sixties, especially before the game-fixing, point-shaving scandal hit. The day D.A. and I saw him at the track Ralphie told us he thought the five horse, Count Rose, would be a nice bet in the first race. The jockeys liked him, Ralphie Love said. D.A. and I bet the five to win, he went off at nine to two, and sure enough, just as the pack hit the top of the stretch they parted like the Red Sea and Count Rose came pounding down the middle to win by a comfortable margin. What I didn't know about Gun Bow was whether the jockeys liked him.

I borrowed a total of a hundred dollars, and Big Steve and I headed out toward Arlington Heights. I intended to bet only the eighth, no other races, so we didn't have to be there until about three o'clock. Post time would be at approximately three-thirty. I'd place my bet, watch them run, cash in, go home. The sun was out, the road uncrowded. As Big Steve and I rolled along in his dusty red Olds, a warm feeling of well-being engulfed me. I was so confident that Gun Bow would win in a breeze that I told Big Steve I was going to put the entire C-note on the nose, not across the board as I'd originally planned.

When we were about ten minutes from the track, the sky suddenly clouded over. Then a few drops of rain appeared on the windshield. Thunder rolled, lightning flashed. Seconds later we were inundated by a torrential downpour. Big Steve turned on the windshield wipers full speed, but it didn't do much good. It was one of those sudden, blinding, midwestern summer rainstorms. "Oh no," I said, "I can't believe this." "Don't worry," said Big Steve, "we'll make it on time." "That's not what I'm worried about," I said, "it's Gun Bow. How does he run in the mud?"

I worried the rest of the way to the racetrack. By the time we pulled into the parking lot the rain had slowed to a steady drizzle, but I knew the track surface would no longer be fast and I had no idea what effect sloppy footing would have on Gun Bow's perform-ance. Due to the storm we arrived later than we'd figured to and I had to make a dash for the betting window.

I met Big Steve at the rail near the finish line. The rain had stopped entirely. "So," he said, "what did you do?" I showed him the two fifty-dollar win tickets. There were puddles on the track. The starter's bell rang, and the horses were off. I recalled the time I'd picked a long shot named Miss Windway out of the paper one morning before Big Steve, his brother Big Lar and I went out to the track. I knew Miss Windway would win, but by the time the seventh race, the one in which she was entered, rolled around I was busted and had no more money to bet. I was disgusted with myself for having lost everything so quickly that day and didn't even bother to ask Steve or his brother for a loan. Big Steve, however, put six dollars across the board on Miss Windway, Big Lar put two on the nose, and she went off at something like eighty-five to one. Miss Windway won the race by five lengths.

Now, I figured, even though I had to bet more money to win less, it was my turn. Gun Bow wouldn't let me down; he was too good a horse to let a little mud bother him. Walter Blum was a top jock, too; he wouldn't blow a big stakes race like this. As the horses were moving into the far turn a guy behind us shouted, "Do your job, Blum! I brought my gun with me today!" I turned away and looked up at the sky. The sun came out. As the horses reached the stretch an old guy next to me yelled, "Wa Wa Cy! Come on, Wa Wa Cy!" The odds on Wa Wa Cy, I knew, were fifteen to one. I looked at the man. The top of his head was bald, and he was pulling hard with both hands at the small amount of hair he had left above his ears. At the wire Gun Bow was in front by three lengths.

On our way home Big Steve asked me what was the matter. Why was I so quiet? I'd won, hadn't I? "Just thinking," I said. In my mind I kept seeing that old guy tearing at his hair. "I don't think I'll ever really be much of a gambler," I told Big Steve. "It's foolish to bet long shots and no fun to bet the favorite." Steve laughed. "You didn't see *me* betting," he said, "did you?" The sky clouded over again, and I closed my eyes. Wa Wa Cy, I thought, how could that guy have bet on Wa Wa Cy?

THE
BACKSIDE

*"Take one of those every half-mile
and call me if there's any change."*

—Dr. Hackenbush (Groucho Marx)
to a horse in the movie
A Day at the Races *(1937)*

The first morning I visited the backside at Golden Gate Fields racetrack it was about forty-five minutes before dawn. I stepped carefully down the main row, looking for the barn of a particular trainer. Piles of hay and manure and large puddles of water were everywhere, but the greatest hazard came when a horse appeared, seemingly from nowhere, out of the blackness, and before I could even dodge it the horse was past me, headed for the track for a workout. Mexican grooms carrying lanterns, red bandannas wrapped around their faces like Pancho Villa's henchmen or night brakemen on the *ferrocarril,* slunk by, somehow seeing a clear path where I could not. The February air was foggy, heavy, like Dickensian London's East End. A horse whinnied in my ear, goats clambered out of my way, great tomcats huddled on the barn roofs. When I finally located the barn, a groom told me in Spanish that the trainer was up on the rail, watching his horses. So I made my way back toward the track, stealthily avoiding the obstacles.

RICHARD SOMERS
FORMER TRAINER

Trainers go to their barn, and one of the first things they do is shake up some of their help that's a little late getting up. They start pulling feed tubs and taking bandages off the horses' legs is the first thing that's going to happen in the morning. Most trainers, that tub don't get too far from that horse's door. Everybody knows what tub came out of what stall. The first thing the trainer wants to know is how his horse is eating. If a racehorse don't eat up, the first thing you're going to do is take a temp. You're going to look at what he didn't eat. Maybe he's being overfed and you might cut back his ration until he starts going back on full feed, 'cause you want a horse looking at an empty tub all the time. You want your horses always cleaning up, to get in that habit; so if you got to cut them way back to get them looking at an empty tub and try to build them back up, that's what you're going to do.

The next thing you look for is sick horses, lame horses. You're going to take horses that ran the day before or horses that worked yesterday and you're going to pull bandages on 'em; you're going to look at their legs. Then you're going to have a groom put a shank on him, take him out on the road and you're going to jog him. You take a horse that's dead cold, that hasn't been warmed up and jog it because you're going to see if he's nodding. If a horse is lame in front, his head is going to come up when the bad foot hits the ground. That's called nodding off. You'll see him nod. A sound horse's head just goes boom boom boom boom boom straight. His head is not going to be up and down. It's just the opposite behind. If he's off behind, that head goes down when the sore foot hits the ground, he's unweighting the foot, the leg where the problem's at. You probably can't really jog all the horses, depending on how many you have in the barn, but you are going to check all the legs. You make sure the buckets correspond to every horse, and you mix up the feed for the afternoon feeding early in the day. You want to have that done before nine o'clock, because that's when the office work begins. When you're done training the horses and figuring out what has to be done to what horse, you go over to the racing office and see what races are going to fill, what extras they're going to use, what races are going to go that maybe weren't in the condition book, 'cause a lot of the races that are in the book every day don't fill.

You mix with the jockeys' agents and pick up hints on what races might come up that could be easy spots, races that don't have much depth of quality. Maybe you've got a sharp horse, a horse that's been training well, running real good, everything's going good with him right now. And you'll get a tip from somebody who thinks that a certain race isn't too tough. Well, you know you could probably win it, you could be one-two with your $25,000 horse because that's his division, but there's another race coming up for him. There's nothing that you can slip your $16,000 horse into directly, but he's doing so good you want to run him but you don't want to overmatch him. So, boom, you put him in there. But if they tell you no, that it's a pretty solid twenty-five bunch, you'll back off your sixteen horse and you'll drop in your better horse, your horse that really fits the race well.

After the barn's calmed down, after you've got all your horses that are going to and from the track, you get your office work done. The exercise riders and many of the jockeys will check in around six. The best jocks come in early, they're the hardest workers. They want to check out the horses that are important to ride, to work the horse for special reasons. The jocks will check with the various trainers they're going to ride for, and the exercise riders will hunt up work. The trainer keeps track of everything that's going on with his chalk board. He'll tell the rider to set his tack on so-and-so, and the groom will throw the bridle and saddle on that horse; he'll lead the workout and leg up the rider. The trainer will holler some type of instructions just to make sure it's clear what the rider should do, should he gallop or just jog the horse. Maybe it's the horse's first day back in a while, coming off a tough race or a hard workout, or an injury. The horse might have an ankle problem you've got to watch, to take it easy on. You set up a program for each horse.

Now some trainers, claiming trainers especially, will work a horse in the dark. Not to hide it from the public or the clockers but to hide it from other trainers that are apt to claim that horse from him; and not necessarily because they don't want to lose the horse but because they don't want anyone to know which ones they want to lose and which ones they don't want to lose. They don't want anyone to know which ones are going good or going bad. They want you guessing all the time because a trainer's going to make his living by playing poker with his horses. He's going to take a horse that's run two lousy races and has got two slow workouts and he's been running him for ten thousand and he's going to put him in for sixty-two-fifty. Well, you don't know that he got knocked down leaving the gate the last time he ran, or that the time before he ran a lousy race and two days after that he got sick, so you can assume that was coming on and affected his performance. So now he's got two bad races on his form, two slow workouts, and he's dropped into almost taking a forty percent drop in class, and you go, whoa: Is this horse going bad or what? A lot of people aren't willing to gamble the money to take him, but if they saw him in the morning and watched him work so easy, not even being asked to run, breezing, bouncing home, well, that would change their thinking.

The trainer knows he's worth ten, but it's hard to win with a horse when you run him for just what he's worth. It's tough to do it there but if you run him for sixty-two-fifty, boom, you stole a race with him. Now when you run him back you can run him for eight thousand and you still know you have a $10,000 horse, but the people won't claim him because they'll want to wait until he runs back for sixty-two-fifty. But even if he's claimed at eight, well, the trainer's collected two purses and sold the horse for the eight. Now you're looking at an accumulation of about eight or $9,000 in purse money plus selling a horse that's worth eight or ten. So you're setting on seventeen or $18,000 on a $10,000 horse. So everybody's happy. The trainer made money, jockey made money, owner made money, and you go buy another horse. Trainers are like jockeys, they're all not as good as others, they're not all equal. You're always looking for the horse you can improve for one reason or another, the main thing being to make money.

GREG GILCHRIST
TRAINER

I was raised in a little town called Fort Dick, right on the Oregon-California border. About seventy-five people in the town. My dad trained horses and we had a little ranch there, so I've worked around horses all my life. All the summers I was at the racetrack. I got out of high school in 1968 and went into the service, and as soon as I got out I went to work gallopin' horses, rubbin' horses, everything. I started training on my own in 1973 in Phoenix at Turf Paradise. I don't own any horses now. I have, and sometimes I still do, but it's just too much of a conflict sometimes with owning your own horses because maybe two horses get in the same race or something, and if your horse outruns an owner's horse, someone you're training for, they might frown on that. So I just really haven't gotten into owning horses very much.

People pretty much come to me now with their horses, they go by your record and I guess I've pretty much proved myself and do a decent job. People can see that you can do the job, and they trust you and you just go from there. I don't want to sound like I'm talking about myself, though. There's no miracle man in the horse business. You have to have a horse that can run, and if the horse can't run I don't care if you're Charlie Whittingham or Greg Gilchrist or who you are, if he can't run there's nothing you can do with him. I just try to run my horses where they belong. I don't think you can have a $5,000 horse and run him for fifteen thousand and win very many times. If he's worth five, that's what you have to run him at. If he's worth fifty, that's where you have to run him. You're probably going to lose a lot of horses, which I do. I have a lot of horses claimed, taken from me by other trainers, but I think that when you go over there you have to try to be three to one or less in all the races. If you go over there and every time you're ten to one or better, you're not going to win very many. You're running your horses out of line. Once in a while you'll jump up and win one but consistency is what brings the owners to ya.

I get up at four-thirty every morning, seven days a week. I'm at the barn between five and five-thirty. We start going to the track at six with the twenty-five head I've got here right now. I have probably eight or nine people working for me. We get the horses trained, come back, the grooms put the bandages on, and they take care of the baths, cleaning the stalls, so we're done by about eleven every morning. And of course if you're runnin' in the afternoon you got your routine in the afternoon, too. But we're always done by four. But it's not like a nine-to-five job where you can sit down and wait for your lunch hour. There's always breaks in between, and it's one of those jobs that if you don't like what you're doin' you're not gonna last long in the game. You're not lookin' at vacations and weekends off and all that. It's work every single day. I take some time off, go fishin' and huntin' once in a while, just to get away because if you don't you get too stale. I think you do a better job by just getting away and coming back. You might see things that you don't when you're here all the time. All of the grooms, though, stay at the stables, and the help does turn over a lot, though not so much at my barn. I have one guy who's been with me since just about when I started training. I try to pay my grooms good and treat 'em good, and if they do the job good that's all I ask of them. They make about a thousand dollars a month, and then, of course, they get stakes on horses that win. You have to have some kind of incentive, and it pays off in the long run.

I'll probably lose twenty-five or thirty horses in a year's time by way of claiming, so my horses turn over more than my help does. When I'm winnin' races, doin' real well, I'm havin' a lot of horses claimed off. I'd rather have a horse in a stall that I could win a race with than a horse that was worth a hundred thousand that they were making me run for five hundred thousand. I tell people when I go to training for 'em that if they want to run a horse over their head, I'd just as soon not have the horse. I've had a lot of stakes horses, won the Del Mar Derby, the Bay Meadows Derby.

I like to go out on my saddle horse with the horses to the track. It's easier on the riders goin' out, and it keeps the horses settled down. Besides that, I just like to ride. I used to gallop my own horses, too, until I got too heavy. I'm not really too heavy now, but it's just too hard to get on eighteen in the morning and still do all the other work that I have to do around here. So you really have to rely a lot on your help in this business, and the better help that you have, I really believe the better you're gonna do. Sometimes I'll have to go to Kentucky or Florida for sales and leave for four or five days and I wouldn't have the stable I have now if I couldn't have somebody here that I couldn't completely trust to take care of things.

I feel that you've got to give every horse every opportunity and that you owe every owner whether he's got one horse or fifty. They're all paying you the same to do the job and you owe it to them. Without the owners, the trainer doesn't mean anything, and a good owner will make a good trainer. If you've got a bad owner, an owner who doesn't pay or an owner who doesn't ever want to run his horses where they belong because he's afraid he's gonna lose 'em, you might as well get out of the business 'cause you're not going to do any good.

Racing has changed, not necessarily for the worst, but I think it's changed for the worst as far as the horses are concerned, because they don't last as long, with the drugs and things that can be given to 'em now. There was an old horse named Gold Seal, won some thirty-some races with him. He belonged to my family; we bought him for fifteen hundred dollars and made about a quarter of a million with him. Every time the horse went to the racetrack he tried absolutely as hard as he could. The last time I run him he was twelve years old, eleven or twelve, but they do things different now than they used to. We used to stop on horses, give them the winter off, but now there's year-round racing, so horses don't get a chance to have a rest and get their ailments over with. It's too expensive for the owners to turn 'em out when they don't own farms. The game has changed so much since I was a kid that it's unreal. You don't find a Gold Seal around much anymore. I figure if I can get twelve good races out of a horse a year, I'm talking about good races, out of the eighteen or nineteen times, that's the one I try to get. The horses get sour being in the barn every day, standing in the stalls twenty-two or -three hours a day. Sometimes you've got to give them sixty days out and it'll save giving 'em six months later on.

The bills go on for the owners, and you can't blame them. They want to know why a horse isn't running, or why we didn't run in this or that race. I pretty much tell 'em the way I do things, though, and there's no hard feelings if they want to go somewhere else. I've always figured that if the owner knows more than the trainer then he doesn't need the trainer. When I hire someone to come in and work on my house, or my plumbing, I don't know the first thing about it. If he does the job, then I'm going to go back to the guy next time. If the guy screws up and it's a terrible job, I probably am going to go somewhere else. So, like I said, a good owner makes a trainer, and sometimes the trainer has to dictate to an owner. You gotta realize that you're dealin' with attorneys and doctors, people who have been successful their whole life, and it's hard for them to say to himself, "Well, here's a guy that barely made it through high school and I'm turning over five hundred thousand dollars worth of horses to him." If you don't have control of your owner, you're in pretty sad shape in this business.

Most people in the horse business are gamblers. Every day you gotta think you're gonna come up with the big horse. I think that's what really keeps everybody going. I'm happy with the way things are going, and I really wouldn't change anything I've done, which I've done some pretty crazy things. I've rode horses into bars and stuff like that, my saddlehorse. I have a good time. It gets real competitive here, of course, and a lot of times there's friction with people claimin' each other's horses, or an owner taking a horse from you and givin' it to another fella or vice versa. But I think it's no different than anywhere else in life. The racetrack is its own world. I mean, there's a freeway out there, and we might be at Bay Meadows or Del Mar but when we're in here behind these fences we could be out in the Mojave desert.

When I was a kid we lived in the back of a horse trailer or in a horse van or a tack room, wherever we could. We were running horses for eight hundred dollars and that wasn't but twenty-five years ago. Now they're running races for three million dollars, and it won't be long before it's five million. It's snowballing like that. Anybody can get lucky in this business. I don't ever think about it that much but I'm shootin' for a horse that's gonna run in The Triple Crown races always. I really do believe that someday it will happen.

BARBARA HAGEN

ASSISTANT TRAINER

'm in charge of twenty-three head, to make sure that everything goes okay. Every morning the horses are tied up to the back
of the stall, the bandages are taken off to make sure there isn't any
filling or any heat or problems with their legs or their feet or bodies.
A lot of people just look at the legs, but I go over their backs, their
necks, their general attitude. I pet 'em. If a horse is going to run
that day, I check him out really well. I usually jog him the day
before and have him shod the day before, too. Sometimes I muzzle
them so that they don't eat and fill up. But each horse is different
and requires different kinds of restraint. I let them have their
grains at normal times, and that kind of pacifies them. After they've
had their bath and been checked over, the state vet comes in and
checks them over, checks the shoes. I usually just tie 'em up to the
back of the stall 'cause they're used to that and they'll relax. Turn
their light off and leave 'em alone until it's time to go.

I'll put the rundowns on myself, the bandages they have to wear
depending on the severity of the burning; they burn the hair off of
the back of their fetlocks. Sandy tracks tend to make them burn,
and ninety percent of our horses go in rundowns behind, just for
a precaution. It's worse in the winter because the weather's bad and
the training conditions are rough and they stay wet, and they're
prone to infection that way, too. And then you have a leg blow up
because of infection, because of a burn.

I'd rather be with horses than people. Most of the people on the
backside have to have that inner love for 'em. They'll talk to you,
the horses I mean, and they'll tell ya how they are. I have that
sense. Maybe it's just me and I'm crazy, but I think most people
on the backside are in fact a little goofy when it comes to horses.
I have a big horse right now that talks to me all the time. He took
me about two weeks to figure out, and I spent a lot of hours alone
with him. I know what he's going to do before he does it, I know
how he's going to act, to react. I know what he likes, dislikes, his

general temperament. When a horse wins and does well it's a great feeling for me, like my kid just graduated. I mean that's what it's all about. There's so many good horses that go through life never succeeding because through our own human ignorance we get rushed. There's a money factor, there's all the racing dates we have, two-year-olds that start earlier than they should. It used to be that two-year-olds started later in the year. Now everybody's in it for the money and says hurry up and get this baby broke. And they're not ready for it yet. There's a lot of horses that maybe weren't great horses because they weren't given the time.

So the horse that's running I'll stay with all day. I don't let anybody mess with him. I keep everybody away and keep it quiet around him. Like Grand Exchange, he's the kind of horse that's real nosy. And the day he's in he hand walks and when he hand walks he has to have polo bandages put on because he jumps around and he acts silly, and he wants to show off. I talk to him all the way over to the receiving barn, where the horses go before the race. He doesn't walk in the receiving barn, he walks around the outside or he gets a little cocky and he does a little dance before he goes into the paddock. I just give him plenty of head, and just let him do his little cutting dance and then he's fine. And he's so big that I'm not going to contain him anyway. I just try to keep him from stepping on himself or on me or kicking somebody else and just getting to the track in one piece.

After he's run, depending on how he's run, I try to encourage him. I try to encourage all my horses. They've got a tough go at it, you know. We bring them back, if they don't go to the test barn to be tested for drugs, they come back and get a bath and a good forty-five-minute walk. They get about twenty minutes on the walker, a machine they're attached to that keeps them moving in a circle, and then they have about twenty minutes by hand, and then just let them stand. Just let him let down. After that's done I usually have the boys soap their legs off and really wash off their feet good, and they're brought back to the stall and dried off. I let them urinate and cool out, eat a little hay for about an hour. Then we'll do 'em all up in mud, just to take any of the heat out. I pack their feet with it and put a piece of paper over the mud so that it doesn't fall out. The mud draws the heat, draws any inflammation out. I spray it off the next morning, cold water over heat. I go over him then, the next day, to see what's gone wrong, and he gets electrolytes and vitamins put back into his system. It's important to stay on a regular program.

Since there's so much more racing now and more money involved, it's made it easier for more people to get into the business. People are willing to teach you, to help you get experience to be a trainer or a groom. It's a big, booming business, it's grown so much and there are so many more horses now. It's really phenomenal. Another different aspect is that we have bigger riders now. It's a lot easier for a small guy to come into the business and be a rider. It used to be that you had to serve a long apprenticeship because you couldn't even get on the ponies much less gallop a horse. Now a new kid gallops horses six months, a year, and the trainer slaps them on the back and says, here, you're a jockey, ride it.

When I started training, I had nothing but cheap horses to work with, horses that everybody else had discarded and kind of forgot about. It was quite an accomplishment for me to try to put them back together and sit and wait and wait and wait and then have them win. I enjoy having babies come in and start from scratch not knowing or have the faintest idea what they're doing. Standing in the gate and wondering when the gate opens, am I supposed to run? And then gradually mature into being a good racehorse and winning. It's a real adrenalin rush for me.

MAX "THE PRINCE" MILANO
TRAINER / OWNER

The track now means being surrounded by morons most of the morning, and then walking over to the grandstand and putting up with disgusting, stupid people most of the afternoon. And that's really it. You have stupid people creating losing situations and betting on them. I mean, that's a day at the races. And unfortunately the only one that ever gets brutalized is the horse. They've bred the racehorse out of the barn, so there is no more racehorse. Now you've got a bunch of ponies and just garbage that really doesn't work, can't run fast, and veterinarians have taken over the sport. So what we're dealing with is people that have a lot of money, that have no common sense. There aren't any horsemen left. There's plenty of horses. The horses are not the problem. In Northern California, for example, there's 800 horses in Sacramento, there's 1,500 horses at Golden Gate Fields, there's another 300 at Santa Rosa, there's 250 more at Pleasanton, another 5 or 600 at Stockton. What's missing in 1987 on the racetrack really is the horseman. There are none left.

What's brought it about is inferior grooms. What's happened is that people have found out that you can have twenty horses in the barn at five dollars a day per horse and make a hundred dollars a day. So why race and be competitive? Plus, what's happened in the last twenty years is the trainer doesn't pay the jock anymore, so the jock doesn't care about him. Nobody has to answer to anybody but the owner anymore. So the game has evolved into where it's totally out of control. The owners call all the shots. The trainer who is buried in responsibility and commitment has got to honor the owner's wishes or they go to another trainer. Twenty-five years ago if you were a bad owner and were having a problem with a trainer, and the trainer put the word out that you were a bad owner, you couldn't go and get another trainer to train your horses. You got thrown out. And what's happened now is, every six people that own a gas station come and try to buy a horse, and they think that you're going to get John Henry for $1,500. The racetrack surface is another thing. Nobody ever used to think about the surface of the track. You just went and raced. You assumed it was good. You didn't hear: It's too hard, it's too soft, it's too clumpy, it's too dry, too this, too that. And where are the young horses? What's the life expectancy of a racehorse in 1987? Minimal.

You can run horses year-round, that's fine. But you take a horse that likes to run once a month, so he can run twelve times a year. That's year-round. But if you run him once a week you're not gonna get the good once a month shot out of him. You can have one quality shot or three ordinary shots; it's your choice. I'd rather go over there for one quality shot. Baseball players get seasoning in the minor leagues; you don't bring him in against major league competition until he's ready. Now, if the horse needs to be seasoned, why bring him out against horses that he can't compete with at that stage of his career? You automatically destroy his psyche. You've overtrained him, made him over-competitive, and it ruins the animal. You've blown his mind. Young horses, when you blow their mind, it's irreversible. You can't reverse this process.

I'm pissed because I like the horse and I know what can be done when they're properly managed. I've owned my own for the last seven years, and I'm still standing on this side of the rail, fifty feet from the Gap, so obviously I know what I'm doin'. The horses make the money in order to allow me to stand here and have an opinion. And I don't think there's too many people can do that. Everybody has to have a source of income in order to be able to own the horses. If you can keep six or seven horses in training for twelve years in Northern California, you obviously have to know what you're doin'. If the only source of income is from what the horses make, then I've earned the right to have this opinion. I mean, it's a slippery business.

If you come in the business to buy a horse, there's two ways I can handle you as a trainer. I can gobble you up early, or I can let you enjoy the fruit of winning. Would you walk up to an apple tree and bite the flower? No! You would wait. Would you bite into a green apple? No! You would wait until the apple is ripe, let go of the tree and say, Hey, this is a delicious apple. Why eat flowers if you can eat the ripe apples? It's fun to watch your horse winning, the thrill of having it all happen is great. But if you don't have horses to race that are in the mental and physical frame of mind to race, then it's a waste of time to go over there. I'm not gonna bring a horse over there that's not ready to run.

For instance, we have a horse here we claimed for sixty-two fifty.

He made forty thousand. November the 30th they scraped the surface off of Bay Meadows racetrack. Now, I have a choice. I can feed 'em my horse, or I can say, Hey, to heck with you people. I'm not gonna race anymore here. I don't like the surface. Because why? Because it's gonna ruin this horse. So if I don't have control over my animal my owner overrules me and says, Hey, I want a piece of this purse. But I say, This horse isn't doin' anything until I like the surface of that racetrack. So I wait and I put him on a surface that he likes and he makes another forty grand. It's a logical game ruled by illogical situations.

A person comes up and says, I really like this horse. We raised him, he's a pet of ours and we really think a lot of him. And I say, great, then why do we give this jock a stick and tell him to dig in from go to whoa? Would you do that to your dog? Do you give a guy a chain and tell him to beat the dog up? Do you put a cat in a cage with your pet bird? No! So why take this horse, if you think so much of him, and give a jock a stick and let him whip him? Obviously, the horse is not a pet, he's a tool. So therein lies a problem. You want pets, get a poodle. You want a horse for a pet, go put it in the park. An owner can't have it both ways. I like the animals, I enjoy being around the horses. But if I take a horse out there and he is by my definition in excellent condition and he breaks his leg, that doesn't knock me off my feet. I mean, I go home and eat dinner anyway, because that's the way it is.

See, you come to me and say you're an electrician. I say, okay, fine, fix the lights. I flip the switch and nothing happens. What kind of electrician are you? You say you're a plumber. I say okay, fix the toilet. I flush it, and the shit goes all over the floor. What kind of a plumber is that? So, like in everything else, there's a million plumbers and two of them know how to fix the toilet. There's a million electricians, and three of them can fix the lights. There's 19,000 horse trainers, and there ain't three of 'em can train horses right. The old ones that knew anything are dead and gone. The young ones don't know and don't care. Anybody can do it nowadays. I mean, look how easy it is! Look at the people who are doing it! Even the hygiene has changed. A horse that's on a medication program is supposed to get a shot at five o'clock. But the vet is leaving at three. Okay, he gets the shot at three then. In other words, if it doesn't fit into his schedule, that's all right, it's only a horse, don't worry about it. The whole game is different today. It's really like the Wizard of Oz. It's a little bitty runt standin' behind a big curtain with a microphone, and somebody pulls the curtain and sees it's a little weasel. A joke.

I'm great at what I do, it's just hard to do it. I'm terribly candid with my owners, with everyone. I've gone through my share of owners. The problem with the racetrack is that nobody wants to hear the truth. If I tell an owner his horse can't run, his ego is insulted. This doesn't have anything to do with his ego. The horse can't run! If you had a hundred thousand and you said, hey, Max, here, go buy me some horses, it'd take me a year to spend that money. Not because I'm afraid of the money, not because I can't spend the money. But what I'm lookin' for is a certain kind of horse. And I cannot go look for a horse. The horse has gotta find you.

You gotta be standin' there and when the horse walks by you it goes, pssst, look at me. And you know. He's got this, he's got that. You can look at his body and assume right off the bat he's grossly overtrained and underfed. If you walk through the barn area at eight o'clock at night, you will find that eighty percent of that area has horses with no hay, no water, the lights are on. Nothing's conducive to the Thoroughbred. Walk through any barn but this one and a couple of others, and you're gonna catch radios blastin', all of this noise. The racetrack is supposed to be for racehorses, not full of noise pollution. These animals are fine-tuned machines ready to explode. When a horse in California is aggressive, he's called crazy. The trainers in California, the jockeys for the most part, don't have any courage. When a jock rides a bad race and you pick him up by the throat and you say, "Hey you little piece of shit, I don't like the way you rode that horse!" he doesn't care. If you only have six horses, hey, you don't have nothin'. If you have sixty, you're a smart ass.

The racetrack I came up at, in Chicago, you had no opinion

whatsoever for the first twelve years. You kept your mouth shut. I started gallopin' horses when I was fourteen at Lincoln Fields. And the sickening part about it, twenty-six years later, is that I rode races. I've been out there and I've won a few races, so I know a little about what's happenin' during a race. And I know how irrelevant the jock is. There just aren't many jocks who know how to ride a race anymore. And this on top of the fact of spending forty thousand for a horse, then turning him over to incompetent grooms, trainers, jocks. That's what's happened today. And the influx of chemicals has ruined the horses before their time. I've been on the racetrack since I was fourteen, and if you put me in a square like this for twenty-six years I'm gonna know a little bit about what's goin' on around here, and the life expectancy of these horses is so reduced by incompetence that it's mind-blowing.

I would appear to be a little bit of a lunatic in my opinion because of how adamant I am about all of this. But the reason I'm adamant about it is because I own my own horses. When the vet says to me, this does this and that does that, I say, okay, fine. I walk in, pick up my helmet and get on the horse, and find out he's bullshittin' me. Because what's the vet's job? To sell medicine. The horses can't talk, so the vet says it's this, it's that. So you take the trainer who's very insecure and says please help me, doc, and the next thing you know you've got a six hundred dollar vet bill and a broke-down horse. So what do they do then? They say, well, let's send him out and breed him. Lunacy.

RICHARD SOMERS

Thoroughbreds are real high-strung. You've got to handle them like they're kids, with kid gloves. It's always the one that never does anything, that you don't expect to get you, that hurts you bad. I had a little filly that was so nice and quiet, wasn't mean at all. And one day I go to put on her halter and she just drops her head and goes back into the corner of her stall, and she gets me in the corner where she's got her hay, and all of a sudden she just squeals and fires, just spins and fires at me. One of her feet got me in the back right between my shoulder blades and the other got me in the arm. I hit the back wall, just boom like that, and slid down it, and I was seeing stars. I wasn't moving but I was half-conscious, and here's this filly who doesn't even know why she did it, and she's bumping me with her nose. Somebody came up and found me piled in this stall and got me up and out of there. I had two or three horses that would go out of their way to maim people, nasty sonofaguns, but this little filly wasn't really thinking about doing nothing, and if she had caught me in the back of the head it would have killed me.

I was always too kind with the horses. I'd put myself out of business before I would run a horse and hurt him. Finally, the disappointments of horses' careers being over so fast got to me. And that's when I said, screw this, I don't need it. I had eight horses and in a three-day period I had three of them break down severely. I had another that the people I claimed him off of had injected with cortisone in his suspensory ligaments. That makes it look okay, but then it snaps and that's it. So I had three horses bow severely, and I had to decide whether or not to run the other horse. I just couldn't do it. My whole stable just disintegrated on me, and I just said, I can't handle it. I'm one of those people who goes in and out of the stalls with my horses, I work with them myself. Some trainers who run a lot of horses have to have someone tell him who the horses are. I can't work like that. Not that I have anything against the big promoter-type trainers, like D. Wayne Lukas, who's the greatest promoter who's ever been in the horse business, by far. You've got to give the man credit for that. He's number one. He plays the game bigger and better than anybody who's ever been in it before. But as far as people in the business who understand, who have a great understanding of horses, he's not going to be big on anybody's list.

Trainers like Woody Stephens and Charlie Whittingham and

Lazaro Barrera are great horsemen, men who got themselves on top by being great trainers of cheap horses, of lesser horses. And now they play the game on a level where a horseman doesn't like to see it played, to where they're only looking for graded stakes types of horses, that's all they're looking for. So they go through a lot of horses to get those. They were good horsemen and good trainers of both horses and owners. They train their owners well.

MAX "THE PRINCE" MILANO

I come from what I consider the real racetrack. You see, there's a real racetrack and then there's this fantasyland that these people deal with. Now, unfortunately, the cumulative I.Q. of most of the people we deal with, believe me, we can't add 'em up and get twelve. Talk one-on-one to a jockey, for instance, ask him point-blank questions, and it'll make you vomit. Get a sharp trainer and talk to him and you'll see that the racetrack will teach you to be a cold-hearted liar with a straight face. That's the one thing the racetrack teaches you is how to look right dead in the eye and lie. I don't like to lie and I don't like to bring horses over to the racetrack to get killed. If they get killed, they only get killed once. What that does is allows you credibility. When I get into a situation that is negative to my operation then I have to hold up, because the racetrack will eat more than we can feed it.

Most trainers have lost control of their barn, and for good reason. They're not qualified to be trainers. A person says, I was with this trainer for a year and he taught me how to train. You can't learn how to train horses in a year. Bein' around horses is a way of life, and you have to have a lotta, lotta, lotta experience. And though I don't know what works all the time, I know what doesn't work, which is better. You have to be very open-minded and learn every day. Filter the good, keep that and throw out the garbage, stay away from the contamination. Trainers depend too much on gadgets such as the laser, the magnet, all this other crap, hot and cold machines. The horse can't talk, so everybody's got an out. He took a bad step, he got hung in the webbing of his stall, he tripped on the way to the racetrack. There's so many excuses.

The racetrack is a game of patience, of lulling them to sleep and then bombing them. The racetrack is a place where you pull ninety-seven strings and nothing happens, then all of a sudden, boom! You win, and the people say, I didn't know the horse could run like that. The biggest problem is that trainers tend to overevaluate their horses. You have to deal with what the animal is really worth. The bottom line is, when the bell rings and the whip starts crackin', he's only worth X amount of money. And that's the whole thing about racin'. The horse was made to run, and he's got X amount of ability. Before humans get him he eats, he drinks water and he's happy. Now with incompetent grooms, trainers, vets, something gets done to hurt a horse's psyche, and he's hurt forever. A young horse has a bad experience, like shinbucks, bucked shins, inflammation of the cannon bone that makes his legs sore, too much work too fast, and they treat it chemically and they race him. Well, that destroys the horse, ruins him. There's a lot of pain involved. The trick is to not have the horse have a bad experience so that he'll continue to run for you.

It takes a lot of money to be a leading trainer. It takes a lot of horses. If you won sixty races, you went through 400 horses. I come cruisin' into the barn about five-thirty in the morning. I ask if everybody ate. I check the hay racks, see how much water they're drinkin'. Check an ankle, a tendon, a foot. Every one of these horses has moods, they're very consistent. They don't know Monday from Wednesday, so they're always in the same mood. You can keep 'em all happy, you just have to be tuned into their little quirks and their needs. Some need to be rousted, some need to be handled gently, some have to be rubbed up. What I've found is that once horses are racing the only thing you have to do is take 'em out of their stall for their heads. They don't really need to train much because horses are naturally ready. Once a horse is fit and conditioned, that's it. It takes thirty or forty days to get 'em out of condition.

These handicapping books, all these books by people who've never been on a horse tellin' you how to bet, they don't mean nothing. They can't know anything unless they've been on horses themselves. I been lucky enough in my lifetime to've been on the finest Thoroughbreds in American racing history, and I've been associated with some of the finest trainers. I worked the last three years of my gallopin' career for Bobby Frankel, who's been a premier trainer for twenty years. He showed me how to distinguish value and to add longevity to the animal. By light training you can race and not train, or train and not race. But you can't do both.

But the game has evolved to where you can't even look at the gamble anymore. Now you're attracted to the purse structure. The Damon Runyon part, walkin' over there, eight to one, bettin' your money, a-ha, I got 'em! That's getting eased out. I mean, you don't get to do that as often as you used to be able to. You have to give a horse the proper time off, allow him to get centered, perfectly tuned, take your time with him. Any man that has a horse that can run is easy to talk to on the phone. When an owner calls me up and his horse is doin' good, it's fun to talk to him. When a person calls you up and their horse can't outrun a fat man, it's very difficult to have a conversation. Unfortunately, comin' from Chicago, I never learned how to say tactfully that the horse has no ability. My father owned nightclubs and was a gambler in Calumet City, and he was pretty sharp, a street man who taught his sons not to work for money, to have money work for us. He raised us to tell the truth, that our handshake was better than a written contract. What's lacking in 1987 around here is integrity. A man's handshake is worth nothing. The racetrack people are a very strange group of people, they just don't have the credibility I like. I have no close friends on the racetrack because I'm honest, I tell the truth. I started walking hots when I was fourteen, and I turned trainer in 1975; I'm gonna be forty years old soon. I been here for twenty-six years, and I know what it is to win. I won't lie to people, life is too short and ain't nobody gets out alive.

It's disgusting that I would be considered a veteran racetracker after only twenty-six years. It's disappointing to have this opinion at age forty. The animal is closed in, the straw is no good, the hay's been sprayed with I don't know what. The people that knew how to really handle a racetrack have died and gone. I don't like havin' this opinion at forty instead of at sixty-five or seventy. The only thing that the racetrack has proved to me in the last few years is that you don't have to be very smart to make a lot of money. I really am dedicated to the turf. Racing horses takes a lot of time, and you've got be lucky, too. In the solitude of the night at twelve o'clock when I'm lyin' there lookin' at the ceiling, I do have an attachment to some of my horses. The fact that they made me forty thousand dollars, or the fact that this horse is gonna win, that I just cashed a bet on that horse and picked up two or three thousand, or that everybody thought we had no chance and we knocked 'em off. I mean, that is fun. To be really honest, I'm living proof that everybody eats shit; it's just to what degree. And I figure a hundred million flies cannot be wrong.

TUMWATER TOM

GROOM

I worked in a steel mill in Canada, that's when I bought my first horse. Thirty-five years ago. I was having wife troubles, so I just said fuck it, I'll do my own work at the races. I lost that horse and haven't had the money to buy another horse since. I've been a groom for R.L. Martin for the last fifteen years. I get up at five in the morning, and the first thing I do is open a beer. Then I check out the stalls, get 'em all ready for when the boss gets here about six-thirty or seven. I go back and brush the horses, take the bandages off. Then I bring the saddle, put 'em on, send 'em out with the boy. Gallop boy goes out and then brings 'em back. I give 'em a bath, put 'em on the walk machine, bring 'em in and do all the bandages again. It's the same routine all the time.

A RICHARD SOMERS

groom's job is more or less all day. Your hot walkers are done by about ten or eleven, depending on how early the trainer starts. By the time the horses are cooled out and walked, then the groom has to do all his leg work, rub the horse out, take care of his body and coat, keep him looking good, like a racehorse. He has to maintain the feet. Mud 'em, paint 'em, oil 'em. So he's probably going to feed at ten and when he gets through he might go lie down and take a nap for an hour or two. Then he has his afternoon work, afternoon feeding schedule. If you have a big horse, you'll probably take his bandages off and reset them in the afternoon; remassage their legs, too.

We used to not have any hot walking machines. Now every track you go to you rarely see anybody hand walk a horse anymore. You just got some guy that goes out there and hangs them on the walking machine. And they don't really cool horses out. They don't lead them up to a bucket of water and let them set a little bit, and then walk them a little more, and bring them back to a bucket of water. You got some guy hanging him on a walking machine, and after he figures the horse has been out there long enough he just sticks him back in his stall. The whole thing has changed. The walking machine can walk twenty, thirty horses for a barn, instead of having a hot walker for five horses. It's just economics. And that's what's happened with the grooms, too. The grooms became really impersonal.

LIZ LUNDBERG
GROOM

'm a groom, but I'm working toward a career as an exercise rider. I'm twenty-eight, and I've been working on this sort of off and on. It was something that I started when I got out of high school, but then I went to college and I went to horsemanship school. I have a college degree in history with a minor in creative writing. I started learning to ride down in Florida, I broke my knee down there, so I went back to school, and back and forth. I worked at farms in Ocala. There's a million little girls down there, runaways from home, girls that want to learn to ride, to learn to be exercise riders or jockeys, maybe to train horses someday.

I went to Finger Lakes racetrack after Florida, a small track, and I hated the winter there. I went to school near there, and I was afraid that no one would take me seriously, about wanting to ride, so I thought I'd come out to California and try where no one knew me, to kind of get started again and get a new start. I was tired of people not being serious with me, someone saying, "I'll give you a chance to ride," and then you get screwed literally and figuratively. I don't know if it's any harder for a guy that wants to learn to ride. Maybe girls get more chances, but you get screwed anyhow. And back there nobody ever taught me anything.

Now this is the best job I've had. The trainer is tough but that's the way I like it. He also tells me about riding, what I'm doing wrong and all. I'm gettin' kind of old but I might be able to ride someplace. And I'll see what kind of courage I actually have. I think I have a lot, actually.

I have a room here at the racetrack, and I painted it, white with pink trim, of all things. To make me feel like a woman. When I came out here I got a job working for a guy. He was Chinese. He says, "You boy?" No, I'm a girl. So I painted my room pink, even though you're not supposed to paint them any other color than what they've got. I'm getting more and more established in that little room. If this job doesn't work out, there's a jockey school down south I might go to, just to get started. Without someone trying to get in my pants or something. One thing that's so good on this job, for this trainer, is before this I've never, never worked for a guy that didn't want to screw me. Whether I wanted to or not. So it just never worked out. It interferes with my respect for the guy I'm working for, or it interferes with their respect for me. Like one guy, a trainer, I told him it was nice but said this is not gonna be a permanent situation, I might get a boyfriend. I wanted to have the freedom to do that. So they quickly found someone else and never paid any attention to me. So many people I'd be afraid to work for 'cause of the same thing. You just can't get out of it.

I feel like a squatter here, a nonpermanent person. I have no roots. Racetrack people are like carnival people, they travel around. I once heard someone say they'd never met people who were more slimy and dirty and lying and cheating people than racetrackers. And someone else said, well, carnival people are worse. So I don't really feel like a whole person; I feel like I'm in a subculture or something. Life's like camping out. I don't have a sink or a bathroom in my room. Every time I've got to wash my dishes I've got to go down and use a hose. If I can't find my scouring pad, I use mud. The hot water kicks out all the time; you can't take a hot shower. If they cared about the people here at the racetrack, the management, if they cared about the horsemen and the people that work with the horses, they'd have better facilities for them. They fix up the frontside but they never fix up the backside so the barns are decent for the horses, and the rooms are decent for the people. The gas heaters here not only dry out your sinuses but to me they're dangerous.

I don't really worry about being a woman living alone on the backside as much as I should probably. If you look like you know what you're doing and where you're going, you don't look like an easy target. People aren't really gonna go after you. I don't worry about it, and I know some people do, and I probably should. If I take a shower at night, I lock the door. If I screamed, somebody would hear me; there's more people around now, during the meet. I don't take drugs, so I don't see drugs. I know they're all over the place. There's maybe twenty-five percent women around here, that's my rough guess, but I've only seen one other woman use the shower.

I have a boyfriend, a horseshoer, and we don't really socialize with anyone back here. We have some friends off the racetrack. I stick to my job. At five-thirty I get the feed tubs and water buckets out. I scrub 'em or leave 'em outside. I clean the stalls and fill up the hay nets. I get the first horse that's going out to work ready, brush the dirt off him, make sure there's no crusty stuff on him, and make him look shiny and clean without doing a lot of work. Make sure where you're going to put the tack is clean because you don't want dirt or stuff underneath rubbing against his skin, so you clean him up to avoid irritations and sores. You pick his feet out last. If they go out with a stone, that can cause all kinds of problems. You look at their shoes and make sure they're okay. They might have lost one the night before, or twisted one. So that's knocking off the horse. You get the saddle and bridle, make sure you've got a yoke, with a set of rings, which is like a martingale. The rings keep the reins from going over the horse's head in case you lose them, and keeps the horse's head from going over a certain height. Or you might put different things on, like a shadow roll over his nose so he won't spook at shadows or things on the ground. I get the tack on the first horse, he goes out, then I start the stall, or if there's another horse going out right away I start him. You have to have the horses ready to go when they want them.

To finish the stall, the first thing you do is throw back all the bedding and keep the dirty straw in one pile or else just pitch it into a muck cart. I usually put it into a big pile in the center, with all the good stuff outside, and you rake it out good, and then you throw your bedding back in the center and put fresh stuff on top. It's a good idea to fluff up the straw and everything, and then you pat it down flat so it looks nice. The horse will pack it all down or throw it around the way he wants it, make his own bed, but you want to keep all the lumps out of it. You put some hay in a corner, or in the hay net, whatever the trainer wants. And you put in a bucket full of water. When the horse comes back from working, you wash it and walk it. You don't want to walk the horse for more than twenty-five minutes usually. Different trainers do things differently, of course. Some of 'em like you to stay dumb, just sit around and brush horses and not ask for a lot of money. Other ones will explain their methods to you. But here I'm encouraged to think for myself and be able to speak and ask questions.

I do the tack, I clean the bridles, saddles, girths, maybe put some oil on 'em, saddle soap. If the trainer doesn't really care about the tack, then you can just swipe it off, don't wash it except maybe once a week, use ammonia to take off the greasy stuff. But I like to do it right and wash it every day, not use ammonia on the leather. When I'm done, I go take a nap. I do the laundry, too, the saddle towels, rub rags, and then hang 'em up. I'm finished in the barn by eleven or so, then I come back at three. I set the feeds for each horse, give them their pills, vitamins, crush them in the feed or put 'em in water. Then I run through the stalls, pick out all the manure that's in there that's accumulated since the morning. I fold the laundry, roll up the bandages, and do whatever else needs to be done, like give a certain horse his cough medicine. You feed 'em, and finish around four-thirty. I come back in the early evening and give them some more water. I'm done about seven.

I rode a few horses when I first came to this track, and I guess I didn't seem very confident, and the outrider—the guy who controls what goes on during the workouts and keeps an eye on what's happening—told the trainer it looks like I freeze up in traffic, when there's a lot of horses out. Then my tack room was up near where the outrider kept his horses, and he had a room up there, and he started making these amorous advances at me, which I didn't accept. I just told him I don't do that with married men, and I don't want to do it anyway. He was really pretty romantic, and I told him it probably wouldn't be that bad, it might be nice, but I'm not gonna do it. And I guess he didn't like that. Now he won't let me ride on the track. I don't know if by giving in to him that would have made things any different, but our relationship changed. He saw me going out with my boyfriend, and I guess he has a bad feeling about it, and so maybe I'll never get a chance to exercise here. But I've got to try, and maybe the trainer can do the talking for me and handle it for me.

I always thought that the whole deal for me in life was to go out and beat the boys, and have guts, and stuff like that. I had two older brothers, and they used to beat the crap out of me, tease me all the time. You know, the game in life is to go out and win, win, win. But who wants to be the best except someone who thinks they ain't good enough? The job for me is not to worry about being the best of all. Then you're subject to what everyone else says and thinks anyway. You have to work on being the best *you* can be. It's gonna show up in your work, and then people are gonna want you around.

BOB DUPONT
HORSESHOER

come in about eight or nine o'clock in the morning. I can't work until somebody holds a horse for me, and they're all busy before then training, washing 'em off and they're on the walker. You can't take a chance on tying up a horse to a post or something 'cause they could get their leg over the tie and tear their tendons up and be useless for racing. Very delicate. If a person could see their limbs, they wouldn't want to send 'em to a racetrack, they're so delicate. I have a list of the horses that are in the stable there and the date they were shod before, and when they're going to run, so it makes my job pretty easy. I just look down the date and I see one, I check him. If he needs shoeing, I shoe him. If he doesn't, I put an okay on him, on the list, and the trainer runs the horse the way he is.

I work for one stable now, I'm sixty-eight years old, and I'm taking it easy. On the whole track there's maybe twenty shoers. Most of the horses now are shod with an aluminum shoe. The trainers think that the aluminum shoe being lighter means less of a load for the horse to carry, but they have less support than a steel shoe does. Now we make our own steel shoes. They're just the same thickness as the other, and they weigh maybe an ounce or two heavier on each foot. What amazes me is a rider could be three or four pounds overweight and they'll still ride him, and that's on the horse's back, but they don't want an ounce or two more on his feet.

I'm in the trade forty-two years now. I cut out quarter cracks, I do all foot operations. I had galloped horses, trained for a while, and finally I met up with an old Irishman who took a liking to me and taught me the trade. His name was Dan Healey, and I served five years with him. Great man, a wonderful man. I wished he'd lived longer because I'd like to have learned more from him, but the bum went away and died on me.

My son is shoeing now, and I broke my nephew into the trade, and I helped him break his son into it, and another nephew that shoes saddle horses. It's been a kind of a family deal. A lot of times I'll check a horse's feet and I'll write down or tell the trainer if he's got an ankle or a knee that seems to be bothering him, so it's more than just the shoeing part. A lot of times I have to make special shoes in the fire, egg bars, for instance, a bar that extends out past the back of the hoof to give the horse a little more support back there. It's egg-shaped. There's different kinds of shoes, like mud calks, that have a plate with a toe and a sticker on the heel, to give a horse a better grip on a muddy track; inner rim front and inner rim block heels that are better on the grass, that keep the horse level; raised bar shoes to provide extra cushion for horses that run down their heels and fetlocks; block heels to prevent slipping; bar shoes, with a bar across the heel to protect quarter cracks; all kinds.

I been hurt plenty shoein' horses, too. I got both knees operated on. They tear the kneecaps when you're clinching them, you got the horse's foot on your knee. They tear the kneecap on ya. This foot is mashed so many times I had the bone taken out and put a plastic joint in there. This one here is about the same boat. My pelvis bones were broken in '59, a mare fell on me. And the collar bone on this arm is broken in two places at the same time. Ribs and sternum been smashed, but they pulled the sternum back out again. I've been kicked about every place on my body. I had a horse kick me when I was under him in front, a little short horse, he cow-kicked me and hit me right in the head with the flat of the foot, and it stunned me a little.

I was born a block from a racetrack, so I been around it all my life. My trade has really changed. We used to have a union, and we gave an examination, and when we got through examining a guy and he got his journeyman book he knew the goddamn trade. He could operate just like I do, and patch feet and sew 'em together. These guys now, the state gives them a license and they just shoe a horse and if the horse can work afterward, why they're a shoer. And of course back then we used more steel, and the blacksmiths had more respect for 'em. One of the reasons I work for one man now is because that's the way I've worked all my life. The guy told me I want you to shoe my horses, he didn't tell me how to shoe 'em. If he knew that, what use did he have for me? He could shoe 'em himself. We get vets here that want block heels on horses with bad legs behind, and I take them down to the shop and grind the blocks off, and they look and they see a little bit of steel there and say, Oh, gee, it's going good now, it sure helped to have them blocks on.

The standards were lowered because the Horsemen's Benevolent Protective Association wanted cheaper shoes. They figured that if they got a lot of bodies in here that people would use them. The guys they got examining, now that the HBPA has dropped out of the picture, the state guys, don't know anything about horse shoeing. They got a doctor, and the guy that's checking shoes in the receiving barn before races ain't a journeyman. But it doesn't bother me, I only got a few more years.

In another fifteen to twenty years there won't be anybody here can go in the fire and make anything for a horse to help him. We make step bars for horses with bowed tendons, to raise them up to take the slack off the tendon. They won't know how to make bar shoes anymore. We weld borium on the outside of a shoe to keep it from wearing on that side if a horse needs it. It's a great big ball game, and you don't learn it from a school. There's no school. We used to have an apprentice, and you had to do it right or off comes the head.

I had a horse back in the '50s who had what we call a chalky foot. You could take and break the foot in half-real flimsy. So I took the shoe off and stuck the foot right in a pot with mutton tallow boiling in it, and a certain kind of iodine in it, so it would soak up that animal fat to give it tensile strength. All four of his feet were bad, so I put 'em all in, and I remembered something old man Healey had taught me. I took a set of steel shoes and fitted them and marked them on the outside, went down to a welding shop and had a piece of sixteen gauge material welded all the way around the shoe. Then I cut three hacksaw cuts, two on each and one in the center to make three, and I drove the nails up as high as I could get 'em, brought them over, and preened that metal in around the foot. Since it's tapered, why it made a pocket. And this son of a bitch won two handicaps in a row at Hollywood Park. Then they shipped him to Chicago, and they laughed when he come off the airplane—the California shoes with the bucket feet. And he won by eleven lengths The Stars and Stripes, the biggest handicap in the East at the time.

See, the steel shoe will last, they ain't going to tear it up; but an aluminum shoe, thirty days and you throw the son of a bitch away, it'll lose its tensile strength. That horse that won The Stars and Stripes I'll never forget because the trainer bet two hundred on him for me and he paid twenty-two dollars back there. My wife says to me, "Where'd you get all this money?" I said, "Honey, I just can't figure it out. People just give me money." She laughed, and then I told her the story about shoeing that horse. I'd never told her about it. Women get tired of you telling them what you do.

KATHY WIBERG
EXERCISE RIDER

I work for a trainer, and I get up about four-thirty every morning to get to the track by five-thirty. The track will open at six, and that's when I begin getting on the first of the twenty-three horses in our barn. I get on all of them. The trainer will tell me what to do with them, how he wants them taken; slow, a little fast, gallop them out. And I do pretty much what he tells me to do. I think an exercise rider does a lot. I have to make the horses happy, to change their attitudes. You have a horse that is kind of sour and doesn't want to run, that won't run, and I try to make him happy, play with him, get to know him and change that attitude. I'll tell the boss if one's a little tired, or if there's a little fight, what their personality reflects. You can tell really fast if a horse is starting to get sour, and we'll change the training on him.

As far as gauging how fast I'm working a horse over a particular distance, that's a kind of natural ability. I can't count, I have to feel how the horse is running. Some of them will be real big stride horses and you feel like you're going slower than you're actually going, so you have to try to judge by how big their stride is. A lot of riders go from pole to pole and count to one thousand or so, but

I can't do that. If I try to count, I find myself more off than if I just try to feel it with a horse.

My parents owned horses, that's how I got started. I went to work at Bay Meadows filling buckets and handling horses, cleaning stalls, learning the horses on the grounds. Then I got married, and my husband's dad owns a farm, and he put me on his babies, galloping the babies. I got my license that way. It's tricky because you have to know how to gallop in order to get a license to be an exercise rider, but you can't gallop horses until you have a license, so you have to learn privately. The outrider at the racetrack has to approve you. He makes sure everybody on the track has a license, and the stewards. So the trainer puts you on a nice, easy horse and you gallop him, really relaxed, and get the approval signed. They'll keep watching you though, and you try to get on as many horses as you can.

I haven't had any trouble so far as being a woman goes at the racetrack. I want to ride races and everybody's helping me, even the jockeys. And I don't think strength has anything to do with it. I don't care who you are, you're not going to hold a twelve-hundred pound horse, so you have to be physically strong but it's all a matter of talking to the horse, changing their mind and doing what you want him to do. Say you got a horse that's being really tough with you, really pulling on you and trying to run off with you. Then you have to get his mind off that, change it. A horse can only think of one thing at a time, so you have to change his mind to think of something else. You talk to him, and then it's all in your hands, how you move him.

I'm finished every day around ten. There's a break from eight to eight-twenty, but you work about three and a half hours a day, getting on and off horses, one after the other. Now I want to become a jockey so I go to the races every day, just to be around and watch what's going on. I go see films in the morning and have films of the day before, the races. I go to the track film room, and I see what happens during the races. It becomes pretty clear to you, it's not just a bunch of horses running. You can pick out certain things that are happening in the race, and you learn from them.

To get my jock's license I have to go to the stewards again, tell them I want to be a jockey, and I have to ride a couple of horses in the training races on Saturday mornings. These horses are two-year-olds that have never run on dirt, or problem horses, so they're probably a little more dangerous than in a regular race. They're green horses that don't know what's going on here. And the stewards'll watch me, and they'll decide whether or not I know where I am out there. You can't be running over people, cutting them off or getting in trouble. I'm twenty-three now, I'm starting a little older than most, but everyone's been helpful and I ask all kinds of questions. They see me in the mornings, and they know I can handle a horse. I don't think they think any different of me because I'm a girl. There's a lot of boys out here that want to be riders that just shouldn't be out here at all.

LAFE BASSETT

CLOCKER/TIMER AND FORMER EXERCISE RIDER

Y ou get six dollars for getting on a horse in the morning. There's only three and a half hours to get all the horses worked, and some of it's in the dark, in the cold, in the rain, seven days a week. You're hustling, really hustling. You got to be seen a lot, to get that reputation. You do people favors just to get on the horses. You want that reputation of working hard and being a good hand. I got into situations where people would want to pay me top-dollar, like getting on three for the price of ten. The only problem with that is your athletic edge leaves; you've got to do it every day. If you're getting on fifteen head a day, or sixteen, or seventeen, you're running and jumping off of horses and you're just really hung tight. If you get on only three you lose that edge.

Sometimes I think it's far more difficult to be an exercise boy than it is to be a jockey, 'cause a jockey, you see them come out of the paddock for a race, and a groom's got hold of them, then they hand him to a pony boy who ponies him around the track, accompanies him, and they never let go of him. When they load him into the gate, the starter's got hold of him. When they open that latch, it's just about the first time that the jock's got control of the horse. I'm not saying that riding races is easy; because it's not, it's difficult and it's strenuous. But you get an animal finely tuned so that he's competitive, he's filled to the max with vitamins, fed better than any animal in the world, he's super high and bred that way. You run him and you give him two days off walking around. The next day the exercise boy's got to get on him, take him back out to the same racetrack that he competed on two days before, that he was beaten on, say, that he was whipped down the stretch on, now you got to contain him. And you just contain him by his mouth. You're 125 pounds and he's twelve or thirteen hundred pounds, and you're containing him by his mouth. It's a lot of effort, it takes a lot out of your body. These exercise boys, they're pretty fit suckers.

Most women I've seen finesse horses, which is just as good. They're not strong and they can't overpower a horse, but they'll finesse them and talk them out of stuff. It's just as good. Get them to relax, where I would get on one and manhandle and muscle him down. You get the same job done. And it's tough to get started. First of all you walk from barn to barn asking if anybody needs a rider. You get one or two, somebody sees you, you look all right, you get on three or four, somebody's leaving town for a couple of days, another rider, you take care of his horses. It's just a matter of building up your clientele. You got to pick up on things right away. The trainer might tell you if a horse has a bad habit, he's getting in or getting out. But when you get on a Thoroughbred and you take him to the track and you turn him to start off, you got a matter of ten seconds to figure him out.

The trainer might tell you to take him a mile and a half, you can gallop him along a little bit, the horse might take hold of the bit. The trainer doesn't tell you to stand up, bend over, what to do with him. You hope the trainer has his act together in so far as bits go, if he's got the right bit on the horse in order to control the animal. You change bits on him until you find the right one. You advise the trainer, you're paid for your advice. A horse gets to lugging out, pulling out, and you tell the trainer that maybe this horse will go good with a brush bit or lug-out bit, to keep him from going toward the outside of the track. You put a brush bit on him, which just sits on the outside of his mouth, and when you take hold it pushes like a real coarse hair brush, just digs into the side of his mouth and he runs away from it, to the other side, makes him go in. You might put on a martingale, a ring that keeps the horse's head down. When a horse's head is up, it's hard to control him. If he runs too high, you might use a shadow roll on him, too, a big sheepskin that goes over the nose so that when he throws his head up he finds himself totally blind. Well, he's going to put his head down to see over the top of that shadow roll. Some horses have very sensitive mouths, or bad teeth, they try to take off when you take hold of them, so you use a rubber bit instead of a steel bit. They can clamp down on it and the rubber feels better than the steel and it's a lot better on them. Or a D bit, shaped like a D on the one side of the mouth.

Fillies are different to gallop than colts. Colts are big and manly and tough and always have to be finessed. Two-year-old colts will rear up eighty-five times going to the track. But a filly will rear up on me one time and I take my feet out of the irons because fillies aren't as coordinated on their hind legs as colts. The next time she goes up she's going to go over. They go over a lot, flip over. So you get your feet out of the irons, get ready to go off.

When you get to be a real good hand, you'll come off the track and the trainer will ask you when a horse is hurting. The exercise riders can *pinpoint* it. They'll say left knee, right ankle. Horses that have knee problems stumble 'cause they have a hard time picking it up, where you hardly feel it, stumbling because they don't want to flex an ankle. It takes a long time to learn that, and it's worth a lot to a trainer to have a good exercise rider. The best exercise rider I know right now works for Bobby Frankel, a guy named Al Schweitzer. Absolutely incomparable. He's been getting on fifteen head of horses every day for fifteen years. He's too big to be a jockey, and he has no ambition to be one. If most riders get six dollars to work a horse, Schweitzer's got to be getting eight, top-dollar whatever it is. He can get off a horse and tell you exactly what's happening with that horse. If Schweitzer just wants to pony horses to the gate, that's fine, they'll pay him. He needs some money, fine, he'll get twenty dollars a horse, whatever it takes to keep him working for you. The pony boys get more than the exercise rider anyway. They have to take care of their own pony. So a guy like Schweitzer gets on maybe seventeen head a day as an exercise rider and five times ponies horses to the starting gate during the races, so he's making more money than most of the jocks without riding races. He's just a super exercise rider.

Everybody comes out to the track wanting to be a jockey. At first that's how it is. Then all of a sudden you can't make the weight and you got two or three years in the profession. You're seventeen, eighteen, twenty years old, and you're in limbo. You're super fit, an athlete, coming out in the mornings riding four hours a day. But then what? Your ambition to be a jock is shot, and you have to decide what to do. Are you going to train horses or try to jerk the weight off and ride races, or what? You put off the decision for a couple more months, and all of a sudden it's two years gone by. You got to make a move. It's like being an old sparring partner for boxers. How long can you keep that up? Galloping horses is a lot of fun, but it's a bad way to make a living, with just a few exceptions, like Al Schweitzer. And he trained horses for a while. You don't know how much you're going to be making, where you're going, and if it rains too hard they're going to maybe close down the track that day and you're blown out of your money. You showed up, and they closed the track. It happens all the time, so it's a hard living, a hard way to go.

MAX "THE PRINCE" MILANO

Horses are exactly like kids, they have to be disciplined from time to time in certain areas, and you have to have somebody on 'em that knows how to do that, and that's a bygone era. There are very few exercise people any more. The reason is first of all a horse has to be disciplined in the stall before he can gallop properly on the racetrack. So it comes down to there's no grooms either that's any good. The horse doesn't hit the ground and automatically he's a racehorse. You have to have people around him smarter than he is. If you get on a racehorse that is totally ready to run, it'll knock you out. You'll need a nap. You can only get on six or seven and hold 'em properly. It's an isometric exercise, holdin' a horse, pulling against an immovable object. If a horse found out what he could do with you, it'd be all over, pardner.

You've got to control the horse's mind. We got a two-year-old the other day who'd never been tied to the wall of his stall. He's always pulled the chain right off the wall. So yesterday we tied him up there for six hours. He fought it ferociously, he broke fifteen tie chains, broke everything. Now, if you look close at the horse, he's cut up around the eyes, around his ears, under his neck. For the last two days now his training has been to stand on that wall. The next day he fights it for an hour, thrashing, gagging, inside out, rip, lunge, pull, and then, two hours later, he's standin' there like a parked policeman, up against the wall. So before this horse can go to the racetrack he's gotta know how to act in the stall. There's a direct correlation between the way they act in the stall and the way they act on the track. Now, where the groom lets off, the exercise boy picks up. When the horse goes up to an object that he doesn't want to go by, the exercise boy knows how to get him past it, to make him do what you want him to do. Says in effect to the horse, "Do you wanna go by that box or would you prefer to get your ass whipped from behind?" So, he can get knifed from behind, you knock the hell out of him, whap, whap, or he goes by the box. Once you establish respect, who's in command, the horse responds to you. You're not supposed to respond to the horse.

If you're gallopin' along and the horse goes to prop, to stop cold, say, at thirty-five miles per hour and shoot you off his back like a rocket, you're responding to him. What you have to do is spot his ears and feel him gettin' ready to prop, and you whack him before he can do it, and you knock that thought out of his mind. The exercise boy with experience feels this beginning to happen, and instead of being thrown off, creates a bad experience for the horse, so the next time he thinks about propping he thinks about the bad experience.

With a horse the last thing in is the first thing out. Habit, period. You go at six in the morning, tie him up, brush him off, put on the tack, take him to the racetrack, and then play a little bit comin' home. He's programmed so that goin' to the racetrack is all business. And there's no such thing as a successful trainer without a good exercise rider. Twenty-five years ago and you were a kid comin' to the racetrack you did everything around the barn and the grooms would show you how to tie a knot, and you were tickled to death to tie that knot, just happy to be in the environment. You saddled up a bale of straw, and you practiced whippin', switchin' sticks. And you did that all day because you were just happy to be there. And the grooms were sharp, they protected you and put you in a situation where you got the feel of a horse without getting you in a position where you could get really hurt.

You'd ride a horse around the shed, if you were lucky; a groom would lead you around the shed and tell you how to put your feet, your hands. You'd do this for a real long time. Then as you progressed, the jock'd breeze the horse and you'd go wait for him at the Gap, where he come off the track, and you'd ride him home. Jock'd jump off, you jump on. That'd be fun. You was in the jock's stirrups, you had a helmet. Your toe was cocked and the horse was tired, so he walked back and you got the rhythm. You got the rhythm.

The longer you went, the more you got, and finally you got a couple of easy horses around the barn and you got to jog 'em. But in those days the horses were broke properly, they were handled by humans. The philosophy on the racetrack was to use a young jock, young exercise boy on an old horse and an old exercise rider on a young horse. The old rider teaches the young horse and the old horse teaches the young rider. And that was the evolution of how you wound up being a jockey. Once you jogged 'em, then you galloped 'em forever. You were able to learn at your own level. Some people learned quick and went on, others didn't. Your size dictated how long your career was gonna be. In the old era, once you got past 120 pounds you could not get on racehorses. There's no way a trainer would let a 150, 160, 170 or 180 pound person on a horse because of the leg problem, being unable to really support that much weight without injuring the pasterns, and because of the surface of the racetrack, how hard it is. But nowadays any human being with a helmet can get on, people who have no idea how to gallop a horse.

Horses now run from fear, but in 1957 they ran because they

were mentally and physically ready to go when the starting gates flew open. In the beginning it was just man versus the animal, and as more incompetent people got into the business they picked up more equipment. Not just whips and bridles, but things like extended blinkers or hall bits, trying to equipment the horse into going straight. In the old days you fixed the problem and it straightened itself out. A hall bit is a sprocket on a spring, and it's like on an axle so when you pull the left rein it pops in and gets a hold of the horse's outside face, or the reverse. I don't believe in all this equipment. I believe in balance and experience. It's all balance. You don't put a heavy person on the horse, or someone whose hands are too small, their arms too long. You do it right. If you have a 150-pound person on a horse and the horse starts bucking and gets the rider off balance, it's 150 pounds of negative force because he's unbalanced. But you take a horse that wants to buck and play, the trick is to let him buck and pick him up on the way out of it, not on the way in. When the horse is in flight doing something, you can't twist or torque him or turn him around because then you're messing with the way they're gonna land. To keep 'em sound you've got to let them land naturally, and then catch 'em after they land.

It's a lot like skydiving. You're flying through a space in time, like when the jock is breezin' down the stretch and he switches sticks, he goes to cock his stick, and he drops it, throws it forward, the horse breezing by blows by the stick and you snatch it outta the air! It's a tremendous feeling because you're inside of a bubble inside of a bubble, and it's wild, man, wild! I can't stay off of horses because of that feeling. I love that feeling of a horse comin' up under me and sayin', "Wow, this horse is nice, nice and smooth."

It all comes down to money, because the nice, smooth horse is gonna make money. The icing on the cake is when he goes over and wins, but the fun is bringin' him to that point. Now you have horses that are undisciplined, all over the racetrack, all this spaced-out bullshit, and you turn that unruliness into running knowledge, give them the competitive edge. Like that colt fightin' the wall.

Pretty soon he stops doin' that and learns how to act and it's the same way with a horse runnin' on the racetrack. He's got to learn how to do it. Courage, desire and spunk are the unknown elements of the horse. It's a lot of fun to get on a horse and the horse is gallopin' along and then all of a sudden in his peripheral vision he'll catch somethin' comin' up on him and he'll get tougher and tougher. Without even turnin' around he'll know there's somethin' comin' up behind him and he gets goin', that's his competitive edge, and that's what you look for. You look first for his physical conformation and then for how this horse is gonna best express himself.

I wish I could find an exercise boy as good as I am, that's why I keep gettin' on the horses. When you take a horse a mile, you got to gallop him slow, and the other thing is, inside of that gallop you give him the signal to change leads, to switch to the proper lead front foot, to go to his fresh side. His fresh side is that much stronger. He's programmed to dig in from the quarter pole to the wire, so a horse that's pulling then he turns up the backside. Well, the trick of a good exercise boy is when they turn up the backside and they're pullin' the hell out of ya, they might just cock their head a millimeter, give 'em a tree to look at, try to break their concentration. Or when you're comin' to the wire try to fake 'em out, make 'em think it's over, just lift up and that's it. And a lotta them'll slow way down till they get around the turn, then they realize you've played with 'em and they dig back in.

The tricks come with the territory. You'll see people now riding horses with their irons real short, trying to get leverage. That's stupid because you cannot hold the horse period if the horse wants to go. The real trick is to have the upper-body leverage with the balance because inside of that pulling they let go from time to time, and when they let go, you should let go. When they pull, you pull. It's like flying a kite. And eventually they understand you've got hold of them, and that's cool. You have to take the horse into a certain zone and keep him there. Unfortunately, now, you have dead weight on stupid horses goin' in a circle. The horses are out of control, they're galloping too fast; all of these horses gallop too fast.

The older generation of horse trainer—Bobby Frankel, Lazaro Barrera, Pancho Martin—would never gallop horses so fast. Horses are not supposed to work this fast, to gallop at that speed. It's an easier ride to gallop fast, once around, that's it. This is a sad thing these days. I claim a horse and get on him, I get all that shit equipment off him. When I get my body on the horse I don't generate any fear, I'm not tense, I'm not scared, I'm not cottonmouth. I'm cool, I'm happy, because I've been around horses all my life. If you get on a horse and you hit him where he's always been hit, in the meaty part of the flank, well, he's used to that. But what I do is when I realize he's been handled by punks, I go into an area that he's never been hit, maybe across the ears, across the chest, across the head, across his nose, or I reach down and get him across his gut. When I reach down and hit him with a stick, it lifts him up, they're gonna go forward. They're not gonna run backward, and if they do run backward I'm gonna keep whippin' on him until he goes forward. And the last thing they're gonna remember is gettin' their ass whipped while they was goin' backward. The last thing in is the first thing out.

Bad exercise boys, bad help and hot-walking machines has ruined racing. Used to be, when a horse was walkin' around the shed by hand and he acted up, you shanked him and all that energy was contained. And when you brought him over to the racetrack he ran off it. Now they flip out, tear the walking machine down. They're rearing up, buckin', divin', reelin', spinnin' around. That's all good energy being wasted, being misdirected. Everything I got walks by hand. I buy hot pedigree, something that when you pull the trigger it goes "bang." I don't look for a big, thick-legged pony, I look for the hot blood, the cross of blood. My horses have to be walked by hand because they'll tear that machine out of the ground. Now some ridiculously stupid trainer will go drink coffee and then the next day their groom tells them, "Oh yeah, your horse wrapped his tendon or broke his ankle or popped his knee, hurt his back, cracked his pelvis, or he turned over on the machine and hung himself." And this is an everyday occurrence. This is happening all of the time. This is all bullshit. And why? Because that horse comes in you can't even tie him to the wall.

So now we've got the cart in front of the horse. We got a horse that knows how to run off. He doesn't know how to work, how to walk. Doesn't know how to gallop, or even how to be groomed. The human element disappears because it costs money. You gotta pay a hot walker a few hundred a month. The machine costs fifty dollars. It costs money to have a barn area with grass in it. You take a horse out of the stall in the afternoon and he goes crazy, he doesn't know what to do because he's never been out of the stall in the afternoon. They've been to the track and back, out of the stall twenty minutes in the morning, and that's it. It's tough to do it right with a big stable, so I keep a small one. I'm too heavy now really, 140 pounds, to exercise 'em, but I have to get on and gallop 'em and make sure they're changin' leads, see how they're hittin' the ground. I trust myself.

Horses work off lateral movement. Left front, right hind, right front, left hind. We start at the wire, the finish line of the racetrack. You go in the racetrack, you jog back to the wire. The horse theoretically jogs off an eighth of a mile, three-sixteenths of a mile, quarter of a mile. He steps into his gallop. By that time he should step into his right lead. Now we're goin' past the three-quarter pole, headin' up the backside, on his right lead. That means his right leg is leading and his left leg behind is the lead leg. Right front, left hind. As he comes to the three-eighths pole the momentum will shift. He'll go to his left front and his right hind. Horses that don't change leads behind is called crossfire. Now they're on their left lead in front and they're on their left lead behind, and you'll feel the crossfire. You can feel their ass rock while they're gallopin', so you reach back and kick 'em, and they plop over.

In the old days when I'd come back in and tell the trainer that the horse didn't change leads today, he'd say, "Well, make sure he changes leads tomorrow, goddamn it, or else I'll get somebody on him that can." But in 1987 they say, "The horse hasn't changed leads all year, don't worry about it." Well, that's not normal, because the horse does not know left from right, right from left. All he knows is his momentum and the way it feels underneath him. And when a horse doesn't change leads that's because he doesn't want to, something is bothering him on that lead. I can get a horse into proper alignment, to use his body properly. I can bully him a little bit and wake him up. You keep poppin' him off it and on it, three or four days of this and then all of a sudden, man, they change leads like a machine. When a horse is turnin' for home and he's on his left lead, and he runs from the three-eighths pole to the wire on his left lead, he's eligible to get caught. How many times now do you see a horse deep into the stretch hit that right lead and surge on? That's the fresh side. So you can think that if you get beat and the horse changed leads, then you got outrun. If you get beat and they didn't change leads, you've gotta believe that if you'd changed leads you'd have had a fresh side to run on.

From an old exercise boy's perspective, looking at it for twenty-five years, is that to save money things have deteriorated around the racetrack. The employees are stupid, untutored and underpaid, and the horses don't know anything, either. It's not really comin' around for the better because where are the good exercise people? Where are the good grooms? And where are the people that teach 'em?

SAM BONES
GROOM

You train the horse to accommodate how well he eats. It's very simple. You train the horse how much protein he can take in, how much he can absorb. If he cannot take in the protein and so forth, to be trained firmly, then you have to train slower. You might have to pony him a little bit, take him around the track without anything on his back, get him to breathe slow. If he's a big, tough guy and he can take it, he's eating really well, he's gorging, needs a lot of water and everything, you train him accordingly. The whole trick of training horses is to train by the amount they eat, to make them comfortable with themselves. They eat oats, basically that's all.

MAX "THE PRINCE" MILANO

Hay, timothy and alfalfa, and oats, being the protein. There are several philosophies on what to feed a racehorse, human philosophies, but most of them don't actually have anything to do with the actual horse. The horse basically needs oats, protein and bulk. Roughage and oats. For racing purposes they need a high amount of protein but for a little more power, to maintain weight, they need a certain amount of bulk. His racing consistency will reflect how good he's doing in the feeding department.

Some horses have never been taught to eat out of the hayrack, so you put it on the ground and they suck it up. Most of the horses I claim are not hay eaters; they're real slow oat eaters. When the horse gets hungry, you stimulate his appetite by not giving him a lot of oats. You force him to eat hay. If he eats all of his bedding, because in 1987 it's all sweet-cut near the top, then maybe you wanna keep more hay on the ground than straw, so that if he's gonna eat all this shit there's a certain amount of food value in it.

A young horse needs oats so he can grow. You want the good solid weight on him, a solid muscle mass, to be as hard as possible. A hay belly, a horse that's been eatin' prairie grass, is gonna have superficial weight on him; it'll blow away and he'll get weak. But a horse that's been fed oats, and the proper amount of timothy and alfalfa and roughage, he'll have a tendency to carry and hold his weight and his fitness a lot longer. You want the horse to stay just a little hungry, just a pinch hungry, that's the trick.

Horses with low-grade infections don't eat. Horses with teeth problems don't eat. Horses with asshole exercise boys that have been snatching on their mouth improperly don't eat. Horses that have been over-raced don't eat breakfast, but they've always known that after they've raced they've gotten their dinner, so they usually don't touch their food all day and only suck up their dinner. You try to do what's right for the horse.

Being with the horse, feeding him, handling him, riding him, taking care of him, it's like breathing. That part of it I love dearly. Nobody gets in that space between me and the animal. Sam Bones is a groom, he has it a different way. When he's sitting under a horse's leg and rubbin' him, and he finds that the horse has torn his back, that hurts Sam. Sam gets sore because although there's that outer crust, that toughness, under that you find that the real racetracker has got a real warm, warm fire in him, a warm feel for the animal. When I'm critical of life at the racetrack, when I have something negative to say, it's only because I'm a friend of the animal. And I know a horse could be here four or five years and instead he lasts maybe three or four weeks. He ain't properly taken care of. That hurts. You've got to bring the horse over to the racetrack to run, hand him to a jockey, you want to have him feeling right so the jock can do his job.

VICKI ARAGON

JOCKEY

This is a rough sport. You get out there you're getting on eleven hundred pounds of horse and you're riding against eleven other riders who're out there to try to make a living; we're all out there trying to make money. You get in the gate and you get horses that just don't stand there quietly, you gotta lot of horse to control, and not all horses run in a straight line. They're gonna be bumping somebody, and it's dog eat dog. You see a live horse and you want to ride it. You gotta hustle. It's the way I make my living.

KEN TOHILL
JOCKEY

I get up about four-thirty and head over to the track. I usually average working about nine or ten horses every day. I'm twenty-four, and I weigh 112 pounds. I have trouble keeping my weight down, I have to watch it because I hope to ride another six years. I been working year-round but I'd like to get it down so that I ride one meet and spend a couple of months with my family. I been married for two years now, and we still haven't been on our honeymoon.

My dad was a rider, and my mom trained showhorses. I started riding when I was sixteen. I had a rough time starting out as an apprentice, a bug boy. Bug boys get a five-pound allowance in weight assignments given their horses. This starts with your first ride and lasts one year from the date of your fifth win. But people were putting me on horses that I wasn't ready to ride, probably because of my dad's name, because he'd been a leading rider. And I had no idea how to take care of my money, I had trouble with the IRS, all that. It took me a while to figure it all out.

It's important to have a good agent, someone to get you horses to ride. You gotta have someone you work good with and who works good with other people. A lot of the trainers have a lot of pressure on them and you don't want to talk to 'em wrong. If somebody says the wrong thing, well, that can be a twenty-horse stable that you've been riding for and all of a sudden twenty horses are gone. An agent makes his living off the rider. My first agent, or the second one, I forget, used to cuss at me if I'd miss a work in the morning. He'd say, "You're dealing with my paycheck, too!" And he was right.

I try to ride a couple of horses for all the stables, try to do a little good for everybody. If you ride for one man, all the pressure is on you and you maybe get to trying *too* hard, and you make mistakes. I just try to keep a good attitude and not get discouraged. I learned a lot watching my dad, and riders like Bill Mahorney and Roy Yaka. Most of the riders I knew when I started out are retired now.

CHRIS HUMMEL
JOCKEY

If I don't have a race to ride till later, I'll go play nine holes
of golf or something, and then come in and hit the box, maybe lose
a pound or two. I usually ride four a day, something like that. It's
pretty demanding, you get tired so I don't do much after. I go home,
eat a little something and watch TV with my wife. Most of the
socializing has to be around the off days, of course.

My dad was a nickel-and-dime bettor, and I started out goin' to
the racetracks with him in Coeur d'Alene, Idaho; they had a little
track that's closed down now. And we'd go to Spokane or Yakima,
Washington, to the races. I always thought I'd be a pro football
player, and I was an amateur boxer, a Golden Gloves champion,
but I wanted to ride races, too, and I was too small for football. I'm
happy being a jockey now.

An owner and a trainer can dislike a jock's agent and still use
the rider, because the rider is his own best agent. If he's good,
they'll use him. But if they dislike the rider, they might use him
anyway because they have a good relationship with the agent.
Basically an agent's job is to be the fall guy. I'm the one who's gotta
make the decisions in a race, and a trainer can take the good with
the bad. I don't want the guy getting in my face about it. I feel bad
enough if I made a mistake. The only team, though, is the rider
and the horse. There's one guy out there, and I'm trying to win.
And I'm relying on my team, and that's the horse. I can't carry the
horse across, he's gonna have to get me there.

BRYSON COOPER
JOCKEY

My father had a barbershop up by Longacres racetrack,
and different owners and trainers would come around and keep
telling him he had a son that was small, they didn't think he'd get
big, and eventually I was introduced to a man and I went down and

started working with the horses at his farm. And then I went to the racetrack with this same man when I graduated from high school. It's one thing to be small, but I have some athletic ability, too, and so I got a shot to make it as a rider.

Some horses you just have to sit still on, others you have to work. I've ridden at Longacres, Santa Anita, Portland Meadows, Golden Gate, Rockingham Park, in Spokane, British Columbia. I think the racetracks are in better shape now than they were twenty years ago when I started. The appearance of the track is better, and they have safety rails to try to protect the horse and rider. The public is more aware of the riders now, too, the Shoemakers, Pincays, Corderos. The Breeders' Cup races have brought more public awareness of the sport. I think that's an improvement.

I move around a lot. You can only stay in one place so long and not do any good, and not only does your pride tell you to leave, your pocketbook does after a while, too. So you move around, try to go to different parts of the country and ride. Last year was one of my better years. I did really well up in Seattle and I went back East and did well back there, and now I'm riding a few winners at Golden Gate. I'll keep on as long as my body holds out. I've had five knee operations now. I'll probably last another five years.

MAX "THE PRINCE" MILANO

I'd say about seventy percent of jocks has used machines on a horse at one time or another. Machines are just a Penlite battery, or two batteries hooked into some kind of small conductor, batteries wrapped with tape with a spring-loaded screw on the end that fits in the palm of the hand. The jock uses it to plug the horse, give him a surprise in the form of a slight electrical charge to get him moving. The horse'll either ripple under you and cut out, quit running, so you stop usin' it, or else he'll take off. He could also go right through the rail on you if he gets plugged in at the wrong moment, so it's a judgment shot, usin' machines. If you work a horse usin' a machine, then sometimes you don't even have to use it in a race. You just kind of jab him like you would with a machine and the horse is so used to it that he reacts like he done during the workout. Some of the South American jocks'll keep their thumbnail real long and poke it in the horse's withers or shoulder as if it were a machine and that'll work sometimes. I knew a jock used to use a horseshoe nail pushed through a rein to prod the horse with. And a rider at Del Mar about ten years ago got set down for ten days when he was caught before goin' into the startin' gate with a sharpened guitar pick! A jockey caught using any foreign object will be set down by the stewards. The top riders don't use machines or anything else. People that think the machine makes the difference between a horse winning or losing are foolin' themselves. It's the horse that wins the race, and only one in a hundred will respond favorably to gettin' plugged in. A machine is a stimulus that somebody uses when everything else has failed, including himself.

LAFE BASSETT

A good rider can really get a horse to trust him, to develop a necessary teamwork. The most outstanding example I can think of to illustrate this involved a "suicide race" that took place in Washington state in the early '70s. A suicide race is usually held at a rodeo or fair. It's a contest in which the entrants—any kinds of horses, mixed breeds, ponies, anything—make a short dash to a ledge that leads to a steep grade that leads down into a river. The horses, with riders aboard, swim across the river, come up on the other side, and make another short dash to the finish line. There was an Indian rider who was blind in one eye riding a horse who was blind in both. The horse just followed the Indian's commands and won the race, even though he couldn't see. This Indian rider and his horse didn't have but one good eye between them. At the races you hear people say that a horse won by a nose; well, in this case, the horse won by an eye.

GENE O'CONNOR

JOCKEYS' CLUBHOUSE TRAINER

I come in about nine a.m., and I have two things that I do during the course of the day. A jockey may come in for a rubdown, or else he may have an injury that's minor, and I take care of that. I just had a jockey thrown from his mount and got a knee injury. I iced him down for an hour, whirlpooled him, contrasted the heat and cold, and made a report on it. He'll see the doctor, too. Whatever happens, if they need me I'm right here.

I was a trainer for the United States Davis Cup Team for eight years. I worked pro baseball, football, everything. Now I do the whole California racing circuit: the fairs, Thoroughbreds, quarter horses. The most common problem the jocks come in with is lower back problems. They all like to come in my room and look at my Wall of Fame, all the pictures of jockeys and athletes. I was in Spain with Muhammad Ali in 1972, working the corner with Angelo Dundee. Ali fought a guy from Argentina at midnight in the bull ring in Barcelona. I got a picture of me with Ali in the ring up on the wall. It just adds a little color to the room. There's nothing worse than to come into a room and you have nothing to look at but four walls. And this gives the jockeys something, to see pictures of guys who rode for years and years.

RICHARD SOMERS

Jockeys necessarily have trouble with their weight. They either hit the hot box or else they eat a big meal and then flip. They like the taste of the food but then they got to throw it up. They're bulimics by necessity. And some of them have been doing it for so long that it's amazing; they can just do it on demand. They don't even have to gag themselves. I went out to dinner one night with John Sellers, a great jockey, and I was eating away, enjoying all this good food, and he was just eating me under the table, this little jock. Then, before the dessert came, he excused himself and went out to the bathroom, came back, had dessert, excused himself, went to the bathroom. And I'm sitting there, I can hardly move. Well, he wanted to go dancing, he was light as a feather. He just kept making trips to the bathroom and flipping.

MAX "THE PRINCE" MILANO

The caliber of jockeys that was riding from maybe 1910 or 1915 to 1950 was phenomenal. Those were pure, real-life, absolute total jockeys. They were no bullshit characters. You didn't go through them on the rail, you didn't intimidate them. When I was a little kid and had aspirations to be a jockey, the trainers I talked to said you got to make them think you like to fight as much as you like to ride. I mean the trick in the jock's room was that you take the toughest motherfucker in there and you kick his head in, and then they wouldn't fuck with you on the racetrack. That was the whole game. That was the attitude. And then it grew into respect, but it was all business when the bell rang.

In those days the jocks made their money gambling, knowing when they were right. Without stiffing horses, either; I mean, it wasn't a bunch of thieves. This was a lot of people that did a job well and the slickest of the slick survived. There was just a whole lot of difference between the attitude in 1950 and what it is today. Those jocks had survived the Depression, they were tougher. And in the '50s even, the horses weren't overmedicated, the jock didn't have to worry so much about the horse going down, breaking his legs. And there was no such thing as a race-track that was too dangerous to ride, because the jocks knew how to handle themselves on a muddy track, and the horses were better.

Eddie Arcaro, for instance, was a great rider. When Arcaro rode nothing moved but his eyes. And when he hit a horse, the horse was in perfect absolute motion with him so that all it ever did was lift the horse a little bit. He didn't abuse the horse with the stick, but he knew how to use it. He was very intelligent, very smart. He knew how much horse he had, knew how to manipulate it. He could ride any kind of horse under any circumstance. He was totally in tune with the animal all the time. And here's a man that lived like a millionaire all his life, and will probably die like a millionaire. He probably cannot spend the money that he has or has access to, despite all the larcenous swines that robbed him over his career, and all that goes with making a lot of money; all the walk-ons, the hangers-on, all the bad investments. I never heard any scandal about Eddie Arcaro. I loved Arcaro, I thought he was wonderful. When I think of Eddie Arcaro I don't think of all his great rides, I think of the two-dollar double I had when he was riding at Arlington Park, and he was on my horse in the second race, and I was at rail level and I could see his arm coming up, and off the outside here he came and he won. That was my first conscious awareness of putting the name Arcaro with a jockey on a horse. I was a real little kid, and the only reason I bet on this horse was because Arcaro was riding him. Jockeys don't mean anything in 1987, except for a very few. Arcaro and them others, they knew what they were doing and told the owners so.

PETE AXTHELM

JOURNALIST, WRITING IN *THE THOROUGHBRED RECORD*

A trainer instructed [Eddie Arcaro] carefully [to] take the horse back leaving the gate, rate him about fifth, move to the outside turning for home, then surge to the lead in mid-stretch.

After the horse finished last, the trainer began sputtering, "Why didn't you move up when I told you?" "What?" said Arcaro, "And leave the horse?"

A LAFE BASSETT

rider down at Santa Anita went into the paddock to ride a maiden, a first-time starter, some Fifi that's raised in somebody's backyard. Instead of the trainer giving him instructions, the owner walks up and says, "Look, I raised this horse in my backyard and I know this horse and I've had her in training, I know how she handles and I got this all mapped out. I studied the *Form* all night, and I figure the three horse and the six horse are the speed horses, so you sit third, they should go a quarter of a mile at about :23 1/5 and you should be sitting in a good position. When you get to the half-mile, they should be going about :47 3/5 and this three horse should die out, so that should put you in second position. At the head of the lane she should hook this horse head and head, and I don't think you'll have any problems after that. So they load the horse into the gate and, sure enough, they went the first quarter of a mile in about :23 1/5, this filly's sitting third. They go down the backstretch, a half-mile in about :47 4/5, and as luck would have it, this one horse starts backing out and Fifi winds up in second place. They get to the stretch for home and they change leads, and all of a sudden this jock pulls his horse up to the outside rail, just pulls it up to a dead stop. And this owner, he's just shrieking, going out of his mind! The owner runs up to the jock and says, "What's the matter, what happened to her? Did she take a bad step?" "No," said the jock, "she's fine. I was doing okay, went the first quarter-mile like you said, and the first half like you said, but then I got to the head of the stretch and I just ran out of instructions, so I pulled her up."

SAM BONES

In the old days the jock's agent knew where the gamble was going to be, he was in control. He knew how strong his horse was. When the money was coming down, he knew. He knew what the competition was. When you're talking about the '40s, say, at Belmont Park, you're talking serious money. You're talking a fuckin' massive grandstand that holds forty to 50,000 people. That's a lot of pari-mutuel dollars. And the expression "Get the money" doesn't mean win the race. "Get the money" is an old racetrack expression, and it means let's fill up a sack from the fuckin' pari-mutuel pool.

Why in the fuck would a man want to be a jock's agent years ago before the jock was assured an automatic ten percent of the purse? What in the fuck was his position as a jock's agent? His position was a maneuver. This was a gambler's game. There's a difference between riding for the money and riding to get ten percent. There's a difference between riding when you got four or five thousand down on a fucking horse at eight or ten to one, and riding for the ten percent. A big difference. You see, it's not so much the good rider winning the race. That horse has to be set up in a race. You have to know how to give a horse a race, which is what these people around now cannot do. To know how to do it smoothly. To where I know I can beat these fuckers in front of me, I don't know about those behind me. I know I can beat those up there; the ones I have to worry about are the ones behind me doing the same fucking thing I'm doing.

MAX "THE PRINCE" MILANO

The races weren't fixed then, they weren't fixed. That's not it. There was no year-round racing then, so horses came out that were routers, distance runners, but the people were smart enough not to route them, to sprint them, run them a short distance before they stretched them. So you weren't fixing anything. You were taking care of your business, doing what's right with the animal. By today's definition, because these are stupid fucking people training that think horses should come out ready to absolutely run whatever their distance, three miles or three-quarters of a mile, they think that if the horse comes out and he's not ready to go a mile and a sixteenth, you've stiffed them. Well, that's bullshit. Any asshole that brings a horse out of a long layoff going a route is stupid. The exception is when it's some great horseman like Charlie Whittingham who has had that horse in with such other good horses that it was like three prep races when he's worked him, breezed him with. So, the bottom line is, the races were not dishonest then, and they're not more honest now. The people are a little more stupid now is all, and they were better horsemen back then.

ARCHIE MCCOVEY
FORMER JOCKEYS' AGENT

I found out that being a jockey's agent you're actually a pimp for a pinhead. You're working for a guy who's four feet ten who thinks he's seven feet tall, who's got an ego like he's seven feet tall, and who thinks you live and die on what he does. It becomes a really strange situation to put up with. You're always on your hands and knees to all these trainers, unless you have a really top rider. If you don't, you have to be humble and really beg if you have a lesser rider to get him on horses. And then you always get turned around by the leading rider; if that rider wants the good horse, you somehow managed to get your boy on, well, you just lost the ride. Let's say your boy rides a horse, and the horse surprises everyone and does real well, runs second, say. Well then, the agent for the leading jockey calls up the trainer and says, "Hey, Jim, that filly you ran the other day that ran second, if you run her back in the same spot my boy would like to ride her for you." So you get aced out of that horse even though your jock did a good job.

It looks good for the trainer's owners for him to get the top rider at the meet. The trainer's always playing politics with the owners, too, because they're after him to get the top jock to ride their horse. The trainer doesn't want to turn down the top jock, either, because if his owner found out he'd done that and the horse gets beat, well now you've put yourself in a situation to where you might lose that client. He's going to go somewhere else because he thinks his trainer's an idiot for passing up the leading rider and his horse got beat a nose with Joe Shmo riding! So that's the name of the game.

JOE SANTOS
JOCKEY'S AGENT/PARIMUTUEL CLERK

I represent one rider, Tom Chapman. Some agents represent two jockeys, but since Tommy is one of the more popular riders, I don't do that. I go and check out all the stables that Tommy rides for, and I check the condition book that lists all of the upcoming races. You can only ride one horse, so I discuss it with Tommy and he makes his first choice, picks the horse in the race he thinks is best for the trainers he rides for. He gets the best horses of the stables he works for. We cater to the people that ride him regularly, of course. Tommy's a free-lance rider, but he's loyal to the trainers that like to use him. Sometimes another trainer will ask me if Tommy's available for a certain race, a trainer we don't usually ride for, and I'll check my book and if he's open I'll check with Tommy.

The condition book comes out every two weeks prior to the races, so we know what's scheduled. Each book that comes out has ten racing days in it, and three or four days before one book ends, a new book will come out. Races are entered by the trainers two days ahead of time, and that's when they name the jockeys, too. Most of the trainers are flexible, so that if you get a better mount most of them will let you off the call, to ride one you think is better in that particular race. Some trainers don't like it, though, so you gotta do what you think is best, especially if it's a big stakes race. If you get off one horse onto another they may not like it, but if they're comfortable with you as a rider, they'll take you back.

I take twenty-five percent of everything my rider makes. The truth is that the jockeys really do most of the business themselves, relating to the trainers and owners, but I keep his business intact. The jockey's fees are set by the Horseracing Board. Say the average purse is $5,000 or better: the jockey gets ten percent of the purse money if he wins; $65 for second; $50 for third; $40 for losing out. That's in a purse for $6,000 to $9,900. But then, as the stakes get higher, then they get more money. They still get ten percent of the win purse, but they get five percent of second-place money, five percent of third, and more of a fee for finishing out of the money on a graduated scale.

If you handle an apprentice jockey, you have to work a little harder. You have to get the trainer to let him work horses for him in the mornings, for free, to get to know him so that maybe he'll put him on a horse in the afternoon, take a chance on him. It's rough.

So after I check out the trainers I go to the racing secretary's office at ten o'clock, when they fill the races and draw the post positions. I have to be there at the drawing because I might have two or three horses in the race that Tommy's been named on, and I have to make a choice if they're all or any two are gonna run. The entries are all in a box, and they have a pill box with numbers in it. There are two people there: One draws the cards with the horses' names on it, and at the same time he does that someone else draws a pill with a number on it, and that's the post position for the horse in that race. And if a jockey has two horses in the race, they say, "Chapman's on two. Who do you wanna ride?" And then you choose the one you want; the other one usually has a backup rider anyway. Usually you know in advance when you're gonna switch.

I rode myself. I started in New York when I was sixteen, and when I quit riding I trained a few horses. Now I work as a pari-mutuel clerk in the afternoons, so I'm able to punch tickets, make a day's salary, and watch all the races. This way I have something to fall back on if Tommy quits riding or goes in a slump or gets hurt and has to sit out a while. I had the clerk's job before I took Tommy's book, and he said he didn't see where it would interfere with hustling book, so he didn't mind me working in the afternoons. I've been representing Tommy for five years now, and it's worked out fine. He's a good jockey; he's articulate and intelligent. If he wanted to change tracks, I'd go with him, and he could go because he makes about $200,000 a year riding at Bay Meadows and Golden Gate Fields. He goes to Santa Anita to ride races too, once in a while, and to Hollywood Park and Belmont in New York. But basically we stay put. If Tommy decided to retire, I'd try to get another rider. The guys always change, and there are new riders coming up all the time. It's hard to sell somebody a rider that can't ride. I mean, there are a lot of jocks but there's only about eight or ten at any one track that really make a good living at it. The rest are struggling. A jock gets hot and wins a few races and everybody wants him; he gets cold and they avoid you like the plague. I'm lucky, Tommy's a good jockey. When he wins a big race, a stake, the owner gives us a bonus. We're pretty consistent.

T | LAFE BASSETT

The job of jock's agent is probably the one that outsiders don't understand that well. They can make or break a rider. These guys deal horses right and left, keep good mounts for themselves. The agent has to be smart. Say a top jock gets hurt and has to lay out for a while. His agent goes to a fifth- or sixth-rate jock and says, "Come on, kid, I'm going to use you for a while." And they'll just die, they'll be like dancing little puppies they're so thrilled. Because the big agent can just get you on the big horses that the top jock has been riding. You've got to catch a break if you're a rider. The top agent at Santa Anita walks into a barn like he owns it because he's got the top rider. A jock like Chris McCarron, who's a great rider, isn't going to ride anything but favorites because he's got a top, powerful agent working for him. These top agents are just like in Hollywood, like Swifty Lazar is in the movie business.

It's different at the really top racetracks, too. At Golden Gate Fields, where Russell Baze is the leading jockey, if he gets off your horse and Joe Mediocre gets on him, chances are your horse could lose, because Baze makes that much of a difference at a smaller track. But at Santa Anita, if Chris McCarron doesn't want to ride that horse, well, okay, Delahoussaye can win with him; Pincay can win with him; Bill Shoemaker can win with him; Gary Stevens can win with him. Ain't none of them are slouches, so the competition is fierce. At Golden Gate, Chris McCarron can tell people what to do, but down south he needs his agent to keep him on the big horses.

Say a trainer wants a certain top jock to ride a horse and approaches the agent. The agent looks at the race and says, "You can have him if you run this horse at ten instead of twelve-five; where he thinks his jock has a better chance to bring him in a winner. So the agent can dictate that kind of spot sometimes. And if the trainer doesn't want to do that, then that opens the spot for a jock trying to make it, who'll take the mount going for any price.

And let's say a jock gets in trouble on a horse, pulls him to the outside and the horse stumbles, and when the jock gets off he's pissed off and beats on the horse, gets hot, and the trainer or owner complains and says, "How dare you hit my horse!" Well, the agent comes running in there and gets in between and apologizes, has to kiss ass and get his boy away from there. He's getting paid twenty-five percent, and he's earning it then. He gets paid for taking that shit, letting the owner or trainer yell at him, protecting his jock. The top agents really take care of and control their riders, and when they get a real young rider who's starting out they tell him to keep his mouth shut and let the agent do the talking, to say nothing but yes sir and no sir. Because this agent is going to get this kid on horses owned by Sangster and Getty and Paulson, the top owners, and the agent knows what to say, not this green kid. The agent knows how to deal with these people, so he tells the jock to just keep it crisp, then take off and let the agent talk, that's his job.

Jockeys for the most part suffer from an inferiority complex the first sixteen years of their life. You're four foot ten, what can you do? The coaches won't let you play basketball or football. I traveled around all over with my father, who was a jockey. I changed schools every six weeks and went through the same rituals. Hey, you, you're in the wrong class, you should be in kindergarten Pee Wee. Hey Shorty, that kind of stuff. Girls won't look at you because you're way too short. So by the time you're sixteen years old you've got a chip on your shoulder. You're always the first guy to punch somebody out because you've got something to prove all the time. The guys who have been jocks all their lives, for fifteen or twenty years, I mean the baseball, football, basketball jocks, when they turn pro they're used to the role. But the jockeys are coming in and having the opportunity to prove themselves for the first time. Laffit Pincay, Jr., the great jockey, wanted to be a pro baseball player, represented Panama in the World Games or something; but he was told he was too small, so he became a jockey. I mean those athletic abilities are there, you just have no place to use them.

And then all of a sudden you quit school, start riding horses, and in a couple of years, at eighteen years old, you could be taking down a quarter of a million dollars a year, like Steve Cauthen did; or at least be making a hell of a good living. Now you go back home and you're driving a Maserati. You've got money in your pocket and you can afford to flip off the girls that wouldn't look at you twice. The kids who gave you a hard time are still in school, and here you've begun your adult life and you're making a fortune. They've got beat-up old cars, and you're in a new convertible. You feel like you're hot shit. It's bizarre, and you're not ready to handle it, not at seventeen or eighteen years old. You may be underage, but when you walk into a bar and they find out you're a jockey, you can get that drink, you're a man now. And you start partying it up and your life gets out of control; the money goes through your fingers real quick, you can't handle it, your life, your money, fame, anything. That's also where a good agent comes in; he can get the kid straightened out.

My dad was a founder of the Jockeys Guild. He initiated the gooseneck rail that replaced the straight rail. When you fell off a horse and hit the straight rail, it was real hard; the gooseneck rail will bounce you one way or the other. The Guild also initiated the jock's helmet, the kind they wear today with the shell inside, called the Caliente helmet, a brand name. In the old days the jocks just wore silks over their heads; now they wear the silks on top of the helmet. The Guild got the tracks to pad the starting gates on the inside. Up until then a jock could get knocked off and break himself up on it. But there is no jockeys' union. In 1973, when I was at Hollywood Park, the exercise riders tried to organize. We had meetings and strikes because we were being paid deplorable wages, yet we were being entrusted with millions of dollars worth of racehorses. We did get more money but we didn't go union.

My father started with the Guild in the early '50s. Eddie Arcaro was the president of the Guild at the time. They couldn't get anything done without Arcaro. My father was the head of the central United States. The jocks weren't getting a fair shake, not getting paid. Management had total control of them. Track conditions were questionable; they had to ride on bad surfaces, surfaces that weren't maintained properly. Conditions on the backside were worse than they are today, for the most part. But of course the jocks in those days were not the most honest in the world; there were a lot of games going on. Part of that was due to the poor pay and poor treatment they got. If you had a six-hundred-dollar purse, which you did, of which three hundred went to the winner, but the mutuel pool on the winner was fifteen dollars, it was far more profitable for them to cash in on the mutuel than it was to win the race.

Chicanery will come into the picture when you're dealing at bush league tracks where it isn't profitable to win a race rather than cash a ticket.

Relatively few blacks are in evidence on the backsides of American racetracks today, and only a small handful work as jockeys or trainers. This is in significant contrast to the period in Thoroughbred racing history from approximately 1875, the year of the first Kentucky Derby, to 1911, the last year a black jockey rode in the Derby. Black jockeys dominated the sport in those days; riders such as Isaac Murphy, Jimmy Winkfield, Willie Simms, Bill Walker and Monk Overton were regular participants in and winners of the Kentucky Derby and other major races. These men were legends in their own era much as Bill Shoemaker, Bill Hartack, Eddie Arcaro and Johnny Longden, all white jockeys, have been in more recent times.

Black trainers William Bird, Alex Perry, James Williams and Dud Allen all sent out Kentucky Derby winners. Jockey Isaac Murphy is also credited with being the first black owner of an American Thoroughbred racehorse. More information in this regard can be found in the book *Negro Firsts In Sports* by A.S. "Doc" Young, published in 1963 by Johnson Publishing Company, Chicago.

T MAX "THE PRINCE" MILANO

he way I claim a horse is to look at him several times, look at his paper, his pedigree, check out how he's worked and investigate his training and make sure as much as possible that he's sound. My plan is always to claim him, freshen him up, and run him back when I think he's ready. To do this, to get the horse, I go to the paymaster's office and leave the money the horse is being claimed for. The paymaster gives me an envelope with a slip in it with a big red word, CLAIM, on it. I'm making an application to claim a particular horse in the tenth race, say, on this date. I punch the time clock with the envelope and give it to the steward's aide by the paddock, and he'll mark down the time. The claim has got to be in the claiming box fifteen minutes before the post time of the race the horse is running in. Once the claim goes in the box, win, lose, or draw, if this horse breaks from the starting gate he's ours. If he doesn't make it out of the gate, the claim is void; the current owner doesn't lose him and we get our money back. If somebody else puts in a claim for him, we'll shake for it. Peas with numbers on them will be put in a bottle, and numbers corresponding to the peas will be written on the claim cards. The first pea shaken out of the bottle gets the horse. It's the luck of the draw. You may have been following a horse forever, waiting for the right time; some guy comes along and drops a claim the same time you do, and he wins the shake. That's the way it goes.

Claiming races are the lowest level of racing. You run a horse to win a purse but you risk losing him. The great majority of races run in the United States are claiming races. I watch how a horse works, the frequency, and if he works steadily, regular, that means that he is a survivor. He's a cheap horse but he seems to have maintained that level of consistency inside of his cheapness. I'm looking for something that's just worth what I'm paying for. Now if he happens to be worth a little bit more, that's fine; but if you're going to cash a bet on a racehorse, this is the kind you would cash a bet on. One that's kind of hidden inside the race, say an eight-to-one shot in the program. Maybe the horse has been routing for his last several starts. What I might have in mind is to give him thirty days off, shorten him up and sprint him. The thing is to catch everybody totally off guard, surprise the trainer who's got him now. Nobody wants to lose a sound horse, even if they don't win, because you lose the owner's day pay, and he's gonna get a certain amount of checks if you can keep him runnin'. I always follow along a couple of horses away from the horse I'm gonna claim when we're walking to the paddock. Some people, if they thought that you were gonna claim their horse, they might let the jock run him out in the post parade, do something to disqualify him from the race, turn him loose in the Gap so he runs off the racetrack; something dramatic so that the claim would be voided. They could have the jock tell the vet that the horse doesn't feel right and get him scratched. So to avoid those complications you just keep a low profile, slip in on them and they don't know what's happening. It's a lot easier that way.

PETE PAPPAS
OWNER

I'm a lawyer, but I always liked horseracing. I liked going to the track. I probably would have liked working on the backside, working with horses. To me, that wouldn't be a job. And since I've been in horseracing for the last few years, most of the people who I've met in the game feel the same way about it. Either they're dedicated or like that they've gotten away from the customary types of jobs to do it. They're just a special breed of person.

I'm a professional person, and I look at it this way: I pay my trainer to train, he's the trainer, that's his business. So I'm gonna listen to him. Why should I tell him what to do? He's the trainer, I'm the owner; he does it every day. I do my own job. So I follow his advice all the time. I give him carte blanche. I'm a lawyer, that's what I do right. I expect my clients to follow my advice, and I follow my trainer's advice. He talks to me about it, and I trust him completely. We own the horses together, we're in a partnership, and I like him as a person, so that takes it beyond a trainer-owner relationship. I think that's important, too.

I've always dreamed that someday I'll retire and just be involved with horses; either breeding them or helping out at the track. I work a lot of hours at my job, it's a hard job and causes a lot of stress; and it's that way with my trainer, too, he works just as hard as I do. He goes through a lot of stress, and when he does all that he can do and then something happens that's not right, he feels bad about it. So I see in him what I see in myself when I do my job. But I think that if I were in horse racing, I wouldn't have as much stress. I like to think I'd be more mellow and relaxed about it. But maybe not, not if I had to do it for a living like he does.

We met just through an attorney-client relationship, and I told him I was interested in horses. So the first horse we bought together ran and came in third. It was long odds, and I was so elated I think I grabbed him and lifted him about five feet off the ground. And then the next time out we won. So it was really good. Now we've bought a mare, and we're breeding her. I'm committed to putting money into racing. It's not really a business to me, it's a hobby, but I'd like to see us make a million dollars! Whatever money I'd earn, though, I'd put right back in.

MAX "THE PRINCE" MILANO

Some owners get pretty strange ideas. During the early '70s I had an owner, a very wealthy man who was then in his mid-fifties. He dropped some acid one day and jogged on a beach, then he called me up. "Max," he said, "I took that acid and felt like I could run forever. I want you to put a couple of drops of acid under my horse's tongue. I'll send some to you." The guy was crazy. I took the acid myself.

There are various tax benefits for the racehorse owner. The Internal Revenue Service allows the buyer to depreciate the price of purchase and to deduct it from his or her taxes over three to five years, depending on the horse's age. The owner is allowed to deduct operating expenses, including training services, medical bills, feed and upkeep; the owner may also deduct the profits, if any, derived from future sale of the horse. If the profits are considered as long-term capital gains, sixty percent of the net gain is deemed non-taxable.

MAX "THE PRINCE" MILANO

I'm running a horse today named Papa John who's in against a poor field of really ordinary horses that are probably over-raced and not really 100 percent sound. In my opinion he's in a field that he can be very competitive with. This is my favorite way to come in a race. I like it when I have the edge on paper because I know how he's doin' physically. There's not that much horse in here. The favorite is a four-year-old who's only won two races in his life, and he's got the top jock at the meet on him, so that'll take a lot of the betting action away from my horse. My horse was off for four months, but it's our way of racin'.

The racetrack is fine. He is a bit of a fast-tracker but his father was an excellent off-tracker. His dam's father was an excellent off-tracker. This track today is pretty hard on the bottom, and the fact that they're goin' :22 and :45 in the sprints indicates that they're able to use their speed. What you look for in a situation like this is who's the snappiest, and I think in this situation we're runnin' the snappy horse. He's been eating really well, and he's never failed to fire. So it's a sound shot. If he gets beat, it'll be happenstance, something that happens in the race. But as far as goin' over there, I feel like they have to beat him. He's the one to beat on paper, and physically he's doin' great. So we just have to wait and see how it lies.

You don't get upset and nervous when you're bringin' over a horse that's competitive and you feel has a good chance. The horse theoretically represents you, so this kind of racin' is fun. It's turned out to be a windy day, so even though the track is wet and kind of muddy it's dryin' up in globs. It's much better now than it was an hour ago, and it'll be much better an hour from now. It's a claiming race but I don't expect to lose him, though you never know what to expect. But if we lost him and he won, we'd get $18,000. If we lost him and he finished second, we'd get about $15,000. So, it's hard to lose money on him since he made about $2,000 about sixteen days ago. We'll find out today what he's really made out of. We'll get a real line on him. One thing they do when they claim the horses, though, is leave the money in the office, and that gives you an opportunity to go buy more horses. But if somebody claimed him then I believe he'd be well-sold, because we have X-rayed his ankles and I know there's a certain amount of deterioration there, degenerative cartilage damage. It depends upon how he's managed as to what he's worth. You know, one man's ceiling is another man's floor. That's the same thing with Papa John. If somebody claims him, that's fine; no big deal. Somebody doesn't claim him, that's fine, too.

In reality, when the smoke clears and the dust settles, you hope to always have 'em in the position to sell, because there is no horse racing that survives. They're not equipped to survive. They're not built to survive. The idea is to make as much as possible and use your own judgment as to when to sell. Goin' off this race we can decide whether to raise or drop him in value. If he beats this field today, due to the fact that it's a little bit of an off-track, I have a feeling that he would inflate rather than deflate.

After the race.

Well, we got destroyed. Which is really great, because it's the classic racetrack shot, you know. We think the first three races today they came outta the chute, go :22, :45, to give the superficial impression that the racetrack is fast. We stepped into our race they went :24, :48, 1:13, too slow; and we got pushed right outside the dogs, which is the area that the horses have trained on all day. It was the very deepest part of the racetrack. The four horse put him on the outside fence. He was five wide for a mile and a sixteenth and got wrecked. Got beat fifteen lengths. So we got to make a dramatic drop, because I don't care, when they get beat fifteen lengths, it's time to go to the bottom and start over.

I didn't talk to the jockey after the race because he was gonna tell me some fuckin' bullshit story that was gonna get me pissed off, and I couldn't stand listenin' to it. I know what happened, 'cause I looked at his form and saw that anytime they go :24, :48 he gets killed. He's not built for stamina, he's built for speed. I told the jock before the race that I did not think there was much speed in here, to let him go and run into the first turn, and that was assuming it was a fast track. I knew it wasn't fast enough because they fluffed it up when they used the corn tillers before the race. The fluffier it gets, the slower it gets. This horse is probably a little faster than he is strong, and when they go this slow it takes away everybody's speed and turns it into a stamina situation.

It rained for the last few days, so we were in a negative situation, and tried to make the track faster than it is, to generate a certain amount of confidence because on paper, in the *Form*, he could outrun the horses he was in with today, on a fast track. But the other races were six furlongs, and the horses were leaving from the starting gate fifty yards off the main track, so they got a lot of acceleration going when they hit the deep part of the track, where it's been tilled. It gives the impression that the track is faster than it really is. So when they break going a mile and a sixteenth, like this race, they break right on the racetrack, not from a chute up off the racetrack. There's no chance to build up that momentum. All these tracks have their own characteristics about them. If you're a player, you learn every characteristic about every racetrack; that's very important. The motherfuckin' track was too deep, too deep, that's all.

So you deal with it. It's a race. It's not gonna make you or break you. But now what would make me feel more intelligent is if I didn't bet a hundred dollars. I don't give a fuck about the hundred, but I should have known better, because if I can't bet it all to win and make a big bet, then the flyer is useless. Down deep I knew this was not the best surface. And that's not good. That means I was gambling, not betting my money. I was gambling instead, and that's two different things. You're gambling that you're right.

So there's no reason to bring him back for the same price. In the race world he was a three-to-one favorite that failed to fire, that got beat fifteen lengths. Nobody knows why; the people don't know what kinda shape he's in. The next time he runs he figures to really fire in hard to the fast racetrack coming off the mud. It figures to take eighteen to twenty-five days to bring him back to one hundred percent. Even though this was a tough race and he got leg-weary today, there's not much concussion when you're goin' so slow. You go a mile and a sixteenth in one minute and forty-six seconds you don't have a concussion problem. The track didn't offer that much resistance, so he's probably okay.

I guess we just didn't get lucky today. It *is* Friday the 13th! Boy, anybody who'd do this for a living. We got a muddy racetrack following a drought all winter. That's life. You either take it on the chin and keep goin' or you don't take it, period. The weakling commits suicide, and the moron gets in a different business. I'm only here on a visit, on the earth, so we'll go as long as we can. It's a big joke because the bottom line is, nobody gets out of here alive. You like to win a little bit more often than we do. And you know, there's two kinds of people on the racetrack: there's the smart-stupid ones, and the stupid-stupid ones. We're fortunate that we're the smart-stupid ones. We think—we *think* we know what we're doin'. But hey, it's once around the oval, and that's the end of the ballgame.

When I first started trainin' horses, I didn't realize it then, but there were a lot more runners around, a lot more competitive racehorses. And the first couple of years that I trained we'd run and they'd win. We'd run, and they'd win. And I used to fly my dad in. He's seventy-five now, but maybe ten years ago, when he was sixty-five, I'd fly him in, the big gambler from Chicago, and we'd bet on the horses. We did really good, too. I'd run a horse, and we'd cash a couple bets. Then we hit a little bit of a slump, and every horse we ran got killed. And you know, you always want to win or do good in front of your father, right? So one day we're walkin' outta the grandstand, and I felt really, really bad. We had bet on this horse again, and again he got beat. And my dad was walkin' along with me, and he said, "You know, Max, we gotta get lucky if the money holds up." I've always thought about that whenever something like this happens. I think, shit, we gotta get lucky if the money holds up.

Two weeks following Papa John's losing effort, Max ran for the first time a horse he'd claimed the previous month, a horse that had not won a race in two years. The horse went off at odds of twenty-five to one and came in third, paying $11.60 to show. Max ran him again a month later, this time going off at twelve to one. The horse won and paid $25.80. After the second race Max said to me, "I'm a great winner, I really am. Boy, we bombed 'em that time, didn't we?" This particular horse, who sweat bullets before every race, who reared, snorted, shivered, shook, panicked in every conceivable way but calmed down the instant his lead hoof hit the oval, went on to win three in a row. The "poor man's Ruffian" Max called him.

THE
FRONTSIDE

"You do not watch a race; you read it."

—*Beryl Markham*

Pubs in the British Isles usually have two sides, each with their own entrance. One is the "spit and sawdust" side, largely devoid of fancy trappings or luxuries of any kind. This is the side that working-men frequent, where their rough clothes, language and manner are not likely to offend more refined patrons. The drinks are a couple of pennies cheaper on this side, too. On the other side there's a rug on the floor, comfortable chairs and heavily padded benches. The room is likely to be more well-lit, the restrooms are better maintained, and the clientele is generally of a more well-appointed nature. It's strictly a class separation, a distinction that, once in place, dies hard.

The difference between The Backside and The Frontside of the racetrack is akin to the division in British pubs. While facilities on The Backside, largely out of view of the public eye, are often tawdry and in disrepair—this is, after all, where the dirty work is done—The Frontside is where management toils, and they are the ones who deal on a more regular basis with the outside world. Most of The Frontside people, however, have worked on The Backside, and some, such as The Gap clocker, the horse identifier, the outrider, the track veterinarian, the groundskeeper, spend virtually all of their working hours out of necessity on The Backside.

There is a curious, if not fascinating, symbiosis at work here, one with more than a few conflicts, as in any inbred society.

SCOTT DORN

GROUNDSKEEPER

I'm the superintendent of buildings and grounds, so sometimes I'm at the racetrack as early as four in the morning, like I was today. We had to seal the track last night, roll it and put the floats on it and make it as smooth and hard as we can in case it rains. Then I had to come in and open it up. The track is composed of about eighty percent sand, a mixture of forty/forty between coarse sand and fine sand, and the rest is silt and clay and organic matter. We try to hold this combination together even through the winter. Most tracks now are about ninety percent sand, and you don't get as much traction on it.

This land was once all marsh, so it's filled in; but if we do our job in the summer, add the right amount of coarse sand, then we make it through the wet part all right with no problem. Yesterday, for example, I went and had a mixture made of 150 yards of clay, 150 yards of shavings, 300 yards of zero-to-eighth-inch-fir bark, and 200 yards of zero-to-quarter-inch fir bark that's been aged for about five years. We'll mix that all together in one big pile and spread it out on the track to try to get it to hold the water, to stop the track from cupping, getting too deep. After the wet weather passes, we put a lot more water on it at the end of the night, and it stays there. The water during the days just keeps the dust down, doesn't do you any good. Right now the track is fast because there's a lot of water at the base. Mother Nature waters this track a lot better than we'll ever water it. With any kind of watering equipment you get dry spots and wet spots, it's not even. If it rains at seven in the morning and we're racing that day, then we're in trouble because we haven't sealed the track. If a storm shows up in the middle of the night that we don't expect, the stable gate will call me and I'll shoot over and start sealing it.

I use a crew of five, three operating engineers and two Teamsters. We just turn the dirt over between races, add some water and harrow it out. That's about all you have time for. I went to twenty-five racetracks a couple of summers ago, to see what other facilities do to maintain their surfaces. You get east of the Mississippi River and you don't know when it's going to rain, so they run on pure sand just because of that. I mean they'll be out with the water truck and it will be pouring down rain. They don't spread any dirt on it at all; they run basically on sand racetracks, so they run a lot deeper than in the West.

I started out doing odd jobs around the racetrack, most of my family worked here, and I just took over grounds keeping about ten years ago. We almost lost the track back then, in 1978. It rained thirty out of thirty-one days that January, and the track just got progressively deeper and deeper. Three days before the meet opened it quit raining. It was overcast for two days, and nothin' happened on the third day; the sun came out and the wind blew and we had to water it by that afternoon. It can change that fast. People think because you have a nice day and it quits raining it's going to dry out, but even more than the sunshine you need the wind.

I talk to the trainers. We've got a pretty good system now. There's a guy from the trainers' track committee who meets with me, and it saves a lot of headaches for everybody. For instance, if the track is too cuppy, where the horse's hoof hits the track and the sand blows up all around it and he doesn't get a hold of anything, like running at the beach on the soft part; or maybe the track is too hard; the representative will consult with me about it and we'll remedy it. You don't want a bunch of sore horses out here, so we work well together. Of course, sometimes they'll come up with some really crazy things that they want me to do, like a time they wanted me to put on sixty loads of water after the races. We do what we can economically. Just this additive I'm gonna put in now will be about $20,000 worth.

We work all year round because after the meet finishes the racetrack is used as a training facility. We've taken the track apart, back down to the base, then built it up again. We've banked turns a lot more than they used to be. We're after more safety than speed, but they seem to go together. If the track is good, and it's not cupping, the speed just seems to come along. So you got to roll it hard like a brick to make the speed. However, a hard racetrack doesn't necessarily make the speed because the horses sting their feet and they slow down.

In the old days no racing meets overlapped in the state of California. You raced at Hollywood, then at Santa Anita, at Del Mar, Golden Gate, then at Tanforan and Bay Meadows. A track only raced six or seven weeks out of the year. It was easy to keep a lot of bounce in the surface. And you had all the finest horses. It's much tougher now to keep it consistent. Even if there was a separate training track available to the horsemen during the meet, that would keep the track in better shape; but they have to do their training right on it. The turf track is good and stays that way because we don't run on it until late in the meet and then not very often; it's easy to maintain. Seed it and water it. It's open for works for a half-hour one day a week. Every other December I go to Tucson and attend a seminar with all the other track guys from around the country. We all have basically the same problems, and we discuss how to handle them.

When we set the starting gate out across the track for a mile, mile-and-a-sixteenth race, then you get ruts going in the wrong direction and it causes some problems. We put in a new concrete ditch alongside the rail to help drain the track faster. For safety we've taken down all the judges' stands except for the one at the finish line. We took all the fraction poles that were along the rail and moved them about twelve feet back; all the timing lights, too, moved them off the rail. If a jockey goes over the rail, the only place he can hit something is at the finish line. Luckily, it doesn't happen often.

This racetrack is pretty standard. One mile long and about eighty feet wide. In the winter we use 75,000 gallons of water a day on it; in the summer maybe 150 to 185 thousand gallons. Six years ago we started a program of re-doing all the tack rooms on the backside. We took every tack room down to the bare studs, rewired them, put in smoke detectors, re-Sheetrocked them, new windows, put 'em totally back together. Now they cook in the rooms, which they're not supposed to, so they mug all the smoke detectors. We put on all brand-new doors and locks, but now they're almost all broken again. We redid all the stalls, relined every stall in the barn area, or most of them. Last year we started redoing the roofs, and we put in new water mains. It'll all be tied into the sprinkler system and get us some more water pressure back there.

In the twenty-five years I've been here we've had a few fires, maybe ten or fifteen, and they've all been in tack rooms, never in a stall. Somebody falls asleep with a cigarette. The system's tested four times a year; maintained and checked all the time. There's 1,500 stalls down there, and the people to match. Three-hundred sixty-four tack rooms, and some people live two to three to a room. Between five and six hundred people live there year-round. It's a fair-sized little city. The racetrack brings in a lot of money for the community, for the city that houses it, and it provides jobs for their off-duty policemen and firemen. It's a self-contained city.

BOB UMPHREY
RACING SECRETARY

'm really a handicapper, in that I examine the past performances of horses entered in so-called handicap races and assign different weights that each one of them must carry in that race. The weights are decided on by myself and three other people in the office. We all give our opinion of the horses, and the best horse, in our opinion, gets assigned top weight, the lesser horses carry less weight. We take into consideration weight carried in previous events, quality of competition, money won. There aren't very many handicaps run during a week. This is opposed to allowance races, where conditions are based solely on races won and purses won, so horses are allowed to carry less weight. Claiming races are set up similarly. I write a condition book, listing all the races we offer for a two-week period. This is a kind of menu for trainers to look at. I try to group it so that we don't have all short races in one day, all filly races in one day. The trainers come into the office and enter in the spots where they figure their horse has the best chance of winning. They fill out an entry blank, which is put into a box designating that race. Sometimes I'll offer twelve races for a day, but we'll run only nine or ten. I write my dream card, but in reality I lose a couple of good races.

The races I lose are due to lack of interest on the horseman's part. Generally you're going to lose the better caliber of horses. Those races are the toughest to fill. So we set up extra races, knowing we're not going to be able to fill some. It's hard to cover everybody in the condition books, so some trainers will come in and ask for an extra race to suit their needs. I'll look at it, and if it fits into the plan, and it fills, fine; if it doesn't, it doesn't, and it didn't cost us anything. Like today, the sixth race has only two horses entered in it, an allowance race for fillies and mares. That didn't fill, we called it off. We had an extra race that a couple of people had asked me about, a $50,000 claiming race that got seven in it, so we went with that. This is Thursday, we're making up the card for Saturday now, and that $50,000 claiming race will make a nice Saturday event. The people will bet that race real well.

Right now I'm in the process of trying to make these horsemen want to have better horses, so I'm writing better races. I'll let allowance races go with only five horses in it, to show them that I want to improve the quality. You've got to put your money where your mouth is or they won't do it. When we're handling more money with the horses I'm keeping up the handle. As more trainers become interested in having better horses, then these fives become sevens, and you can make a whole better racing program. It's tough to sort through four $12,500 maiden races a day, and those are tough to bet, too.

The people who run their horses get the stalls, and that's a battle every meet. You have 3,000 applied for for only 1,500 spots. It's up to me to fairly distribute these stalls. I want horses most suited to my racing program. They're going to help me and racing the most. You try to get horses that are ready. You don't want to give the guy ten stalls for ten maiden twelve-fives. It's a constant problem, weeding out the bad horses.

LAFE BASSETT

'm on the stabling committee, and if a trainer has horses that are coming off a long layoff or maidens that have no form to 'em, then we want to see a work pattern; as head clocker that's my department. We also want to delegate stalls for horses that will be here, on the grounds, not stabled at another racetrack with the possibility that he'll be shipped here. Of course, if a great horse wants to come here and run, if the trainer needs a stall for him, of course we'll accommodate him. Naturally the trainers who run more horses more often will get more stalls. The big outfits. The little outfits, the guy who has maybe four- or five-head of horses but who runs eighteen times during the meet and he only won two, but hell, he was ninth, second nine times, and third six times, he's got an eighty percent in-the-money pattern. That's good and productive for a little outfit. You got to take that into consideration, even if he's not running the horses that are the favorites. There's a spot for him on the grounds.

The racing secretary is interested in the number of starts. If you're not in the win columns, percentage-wise, across the board, in the money, he wants you out. He wants those stalls being productive. A guy can have a big turnover in his stalls, have horses coming and going, but that's all right as long as he fills the stalls and runs his horses. You can't expect to use the racetrack as a training track for horses that don't run in the afternoon.

BOB UMPHREY

I'm a racetrack brat. I'm thirty-four now, and my dad's still a trainer, based in Florida. I planned to be a trainer but my dad talked me out of it, he didn't want me rubbin' horses. He wanted me to do something better with my life. A trainer has to work seven days a week, cater to his owners, sick horses and pick up the pieces of his broken dreams. I can go home at night and go to sleep. So I went to college and graduated in marketing from the University of Florida.

I've been the racing secretary at Hollywood Park, Arlington Park, Gulfstream Park, Laurel and Golden Gate Fields and Bay Meadows. In California it's important to write races for Cal-breds only, horses from California only, as an incentive program to put money back into the industry. In these races the California breeder gets ten percent of the purse, the jockey gets ten percent, the trainer gets ten percent, and the owner gets the rest, out of which he pays his expenses. The racetrack does not share in any of that. We make our money from the handle, the money bet on the race.

The "overnights" are races other than stakes races. Stakes money is taken out at the beginning of a meet. A certain amount of money per day will go into the stakes program, that's set in advance; and it's up to me to juggle the rest of the money into the overnights. I love turf races, and the fans love 'em, and they draw horses from all over because some horses will run only on the turf. You get more variety using both dirt and turf for races. But what I have to do is set up races that people are gonna bet the most money on. I'm not here to work for the trainers, and when I have to cancel a race that someone had a horse entered in, and he really wanted to run it, well, that's too bad. I have to substitute what looks like a better betting race, and that makes some trainers unhappy. It's bound to happen. A bad race on Saturday, for instance, can cost us who knows how much money. You try to hit 'em with your best shot on Saturday, that's our largest day.

More satellite track-wagering sites are coming into being in California, and that's increasing the handle as well as increasing purses. Southern California has the best horses year-round. On the top level there's the New York Racing Association, Belmont, Aqueduct, Saratoga; the Florida winter dates; the Santa Anita meet, Hollywood Park meet, and the Del Mar meet. Then comes the second echelon: Bay Meadows, Golden Gate Fields, Monmouth Park, Louisiana Downs. Then a step below them is Philadelphia racing, Maryland racing, all the way down to Charles Town, that's the end of the road. There are over a hundred racetracks in the United States, so you have several levels of racing.

The idea I keep in mind in writing races wherever I am is to handicap so that the horses are going to be even on the wire. I think weight is more in the minds of the trainers than it is in my mind. I think if a horse is ready to run and he's not carrying an exorbitant amount of weight going a long distance, he's going to win regardless if he's the better horse. At 122 pounds going six furlongs I don't think's gonna adversely affect a good horse. If you're talkin' 131 pounds going a mile and a quarter against the best horses in the world, giving them seven or eight pounds, then you have a slight problem. Then the weight can tell.

Trainers come in and beef all the time about how much weight is assigned to his horse, that's a constant. But I just say, "If you don't like it, you don't run. Apparently I think more of your horse than you do." That always stops 'em!

PETER TUNNEY
GENERAL MANAGER

The managerial role is one of coordinating department heads, the overall supervision of the racing operation. I mean managing the frontside as well as the backside, because I maintain the controlling interest in that racing office supervision, and entries. Preparatory work involves contracts and hiring, interviewing personnel prior to the meet starting. Once the meet is underway it's more of a crisis management situation. You hope everything is in place. I try to spend time all around the racing plant, walking around, seeing people, talking to patrons. I like to get feedback from patrons. I like to know if they're getting what they want. Are they comfortable, do they have any beefs. It's important to constantly be improving the facility, and it takes money to make money. If we're going to give the fans something that's convenient, comfortable, the proper amenities, you're going to have to spend money to do that for him.

The backside is just as important. You try to make it clean and comfortable for them when they come in every year. The barns are of wood construction, so doors and hinges get broken, stalls get kicked in, tackrooms get vandalized. We have to maintain it properly and make repairs, to upgrade constantly. And we have to upgrade the types and classes of horses. It's my philosophy that if you can get better-quality horses, stables, trainers, that it creates more excitement and the fans have a tendency to wager more on that competitiveness than they do on a more humdrum program.

Intertrack wagering and the state lottery began at about the same time in California and there was an immediate decline in racetrack attendance. Perhaps as much as ten percent but probably more in the area of five to seven percent. This is not unique in areas where racing has existed and the lottery has come in. The lottery tends to make an initial impact and then as people see what the odds on winning are, it slacks off. At the racetrack at least you've got a pretty good shot at picking a winner and controlling to a certain degree your destiny. You choose the horse and the jockey, as opposed to the lottery where you pick a number. My job is to get people out to the racetrack.

I've been in racing all my life. I'm forty-eight now, so for thirty years. My father was a steward at Southern California tracks, and my uncle ran Del Mar, back when Bing Crosby and Pat O'Brien owned the track. I worked in the parking lot, sold admissions, worked on the backside as a hot walker, helped around the barns. I moved onto the frontside and eventually became a steward and a racing secretary. I work very closely with the racing secretary. I spend about an hour each morning in the stable area, I oversee the pari-mutuel operation, talk with the mutuel manager, check up on the sports medicine operation we have now. I move around the track as much as I can. The toughest thing I have to contend with, though, is apathy. We get into a daily routine here, and I have to encourage department heads to move around the facility, supervise the individuals under them, make themselves available for the fans, and convince the employees to give first-class service to the patron.

One thing I do discourage is gambling by the track employees. I frown on that. It's always interesting to me when people talk about the per capita, the number of people that go through the gate divided by the amount of money wagered per day. Generally it comes out that if you've got ten thousand people in the facility, they're going to wager about two million. It's a two hundred dollar per capita. No one has ever stopped to take the time to ask how much of the handle is comprised of employee wagering. I'm not naive. I've grown up from the time I was fifteen working in the parking lot at Santa Anita where a runner was coming around out there collecting bets from the parking lot guys. Not that it was conflicting with their jobs, but everybody knew exactly where they were in the day, that the second race was just about to run, and it was the second half of the daily double and the three horse won the first race. I mean, everybody knows, there's no secrets. There's an old saying: Why does so-and-so work at the racetrack? Because he gets in free.

There's no question that our employees have a particular interest in the outcome of the races. We've had some employee disciplinary problems and disciplinary actions as a result of it. I frown on it for two reasons: One, people that are trying to do their jobs, and are worried about the outcome of the races, are not properly fulfilling the job that we're paying them for. Two, I think over a period of time with mutuel clerks if they've just bet a race and their horse loses, and then a patron comes running up to their window to collect and throws down his tickets and he's all excited, I think it creates a kind of animosity on the part of the mutuel clerk. That concerns me because he should really be saying to the patron, "I'm glad you won. Do you want to bet on the next race?" Or, "That's great. I'll see you a little later." They should create the atmosphere that you have when you drive into Disneyland or Dodger Stadium. The main interest of the employee should be to make this place a better place for the patron. I'm not suggesting that we're trying to make this a Disneyland, but I am saying that if our employees are betting on the races and losing that's going to affect how they behave.

We supervise the mutuel clerks closely; actually, they supervise themselves, within their own department, which is unionized, so it's not management-union. Other than the mutuel manager all of the people who work in the mutuel department are union brothers. A good mutuel clerk does not like bearing the stigma caused by a bad clerk. There was a mutuel clerk at Del Mar a couple of years ago who went $30,000 short in one day. He bet throughout the day, giving himself tickets, and before he knew it he was thirty thousand in the hole. In just one day. There was an indictment, and the case went to court. That has to be treated severely. It's a great temptation to take tickets on a cinch in the eighth race, bet him to win, and then he runs second, like the fellow at Del Mar did. Then he came back in the ninth race and bet a number of exactas, the horses that will finish one-two, baseballed them, bet them in combinations, to try to make up his losses, they ran out, and he was even deeper in the hole.

We're here to provide entertainment and make money. We get our percentage just like the casinos. We take seventeen cents out of every dollar. Five cents goes to the horseman; five cents goes to the state, which is a bit of a sore subject with me because they have no vested interest; and the rest to the racetrack. So we really are three partners in this. If you abuse the betting patron, abuse him to the degree that he's going to have less of a chance to win some money, then I think in the long run the business is going to go downhill. You have to treat the fellow right.

BEN LARRAINE
OUTRIDER

I come in about five-thirty and saddle up. I make sure the doors to the racing strip are opened at two minutes to six, when the workouts begin. I'm the baby-sitter, the lifeguard. I make sure the riders follow the rules, make sure people do the right things and conduct themselves in a careful manner. I'm in charge of the safety of the racecourse. When riders do not follow regular procedure, I make a complaint to the steward; and every time someone gets dumped, hurt or there's loose horses, I'm the one who checks the horses and directs the traffic inside the racetrack.

There are not really too many rules. You do not gallop the wrong way; you cannot gallop clockwise. You can *jog* clockwise. And you don't gallop on the rail with horses that are working; that means better than a two-minute clip, faster than at a two-minute clip. If somebody repeats the offense three or four times in a short period of time, I exercise my better judgment and make a formal complaint. Nine out of ten times the rider gets fined. I always notify the rider the first time he does something wrong. I have a list that I carry around all the time, and I tell him if his attitude doesn't change I'll take him to the commissioners.

Some trainers like to jog horses the wrong way four, five days, even two weeks in a row. Horses jog so much the wrong way that they get to the point they want to do something else, so it's hard to keep them jogging anymore. They start loping. The exercise riders want to save a little time in order to get a couple more horses in the morning, so they cheat every time; at least a handful of them do, maybe a dozen out of 150 riders. Otherwise, it's pretty easy going.

I work hard at training my own horse that I ride, a quarter horse. He must be able to respond without much command, instantly, when we're in a tight situation where loose horses are on the track. I come from a family of ranchers in Chile. My father had arroyo horses, rodeo horses, on a big hacienda. At two and a half, three years old, I learned how to mount, and by twelve or fourteen I started getting assigned jobs on the ranch. I went to a military academy where I learned the English horse, learned dressage, and I played polo for a year. I came to the States twenty years ago and started galloping horses. I groomed for about six years, I went back to Chile for three years, and then came back here, bought my first pony, and went into the pony business, accompanying the racehorses.

One day at the racetrack the outrider got sick and didn't show up, so I was asked to cover for him. Pretty soon it became a routine, substituting. Then the steady guy got hurt, took a spill and ended up in the hospital for a long time, and he gave it up. The job fell to me, and I took it.

Every individual horse, when it gets loose, has a different speed and a different state of mind. It's a different situation each time: left side, right side, middle of the track. You've got to grab the horse by reflex. You don't want to pin the horse on the rail because then he'll go over it. You have to rate him and make sure that you're getting up enough speed so that when he comes to you you'll stop together. If he goes faster than you, then when you grab him you wind up pulling him in front of the pony and you'll do a somersault out of the saddle. If you're going faster than him, most likely he'll duck behind your pony. If you squeeze him too much, he'll go behind your pony, he'll pin you on the rail. Running them down becomes natural. If a horse gets loose, loses a rider, a red light goes on at each post around the track, a warning light. The most dangerous situation is when a loose horse runs off the track through the Gap into the barn area and starts running over people.

I believe that the best way is to turn your horse in the same direction the loose horse is going. You never face a loose horse. Always have your back to him in the middle of the racetrack, and that way the loose horse and the outrider can operate around you. Riders on the track should not zig zag or try to guess which way the loose horse is coming. There will be a wreck that way. The loose horse doesn't wreck anyone, it's the people that get in the way. Loose horses will duck you every time.

A real problem is when the rider gets in trouble: He breaks a rein or a stirrup, gets hung up in the stirrup and you go after him. That's when you got to put your neck on the line. If a rider's on a young horse and a stirrup breaks, the horse might duck, or more likely put him over the rail. In really tough situations I've got maybe three seconds to react. I'm just sitting here on my horse and somebody yells. You got to go *now!*

But this is not a very popular job, because you're policing the riders as well as looking out for their safety. These people are friends of mine, and unfortunately I have to fine a few every week, so it's pretty tough that way, and I hate to do it. I mean, yes, they're my friends, but they're always trying to pull a fast one on me anyway. That's their nature. Anyone who hasn't tried to deceive the outrider is not a horseman!

BUCK LAWN
CLOCKER

To be a clocker, to time the morning workouts, you need a knowledge of racing, of being around horses, in order to understand how to do the job. You don't just take somebody out of the parking lot and have him do it. It can be learned, but it's a lot better if you understand the animal. You have to know that some horses will come out in the morning and only jog, trot, they'll gallop, and we don't time them. When horses work, they'll line up at the pole, move to the inside. As a clocker you're always looking for motion, degrees of motion. You have to develop an instinct for seeing a horse moving on the racetrack in a way that suggests he's going to run. You have to know what pole is what: If he's over at the far turn and he's at the green and white pole, then he's working three-eighths of a mile; if he's in the middle of the backstretch or at the red and white pole, then he's working a half-mile; or he's working five-eighths, and so on, like that. Just like knowing the frets on a guitar. The times the horses run are going to be recorded and they'll be printed in the *Racing Form,* which the bettors will use as gauges, as information to guide them in their handicapping. The thing is that horses are unpredictable; some are phlegmatic in their workouts and may run better in the afternoon; others are precocious and just never live up to their superior works. The works may not really have a great deal to do with what the horse's actual performance in a race will be.

Most of the time the clockers, who are sitting above the grandstand in the stewards' reviewing booth, will be given a cue that a horse is going to work by an identifier at the Gap, the place where the horses come onto the track from the backside. There'll be maybe thirty horses running around down there and there's two or three clockers, and of course more than one horse is going to be working at the same time, so the clockers have to be able to communicate with each other and keep track of every horse.

LAFE BASSETT
HEAD CLOCKER

California horseracing law states that all horses must be identified by name prior to working. That's not a law that's highly enforced anyplace else, but it is in California. We start at six A.M., when the track opens, and it goes on until ten, every day of the week. The first forty-five minutes it's pretty difficult to see. We catch as much as we can but it's possible to miss horses real early in the morning. It's usually the big outfits that work real early because they have so many horses it'd be impossible to get them all in otherwise. All works are recorded and an alphabetical listing is published. The workout times are made public. The bettors get them, the trainers get them, the *Racing Form* gets them. All of the horses are registered, their names are in the Thoroughbred book, and we've got to make an accurate identification of them. Every clocker keeps a book on the horses that are stabled at the racetrack with his own code for identifying the horse. If a horse is trained by Salazar, say, the clocker has a Salazar list in his book, and Salazar has a dark bay colt named Huelo Blue who's got a pointed star on his forehead. We check the registry and see that the colt is a three-year-old, he's registered, so he's okay. We write down the colt's name and put a pointed star to the right. All the horses on the grounds are i.d.'ed like this, so when we get a name of a horse from a trainer it better coincide with what we've got.

S BUCK LAWN

o now the horses are all warmed up, and they're all heading to posts. So I say, I got the five. That means I got a horse leaving the five. I'll let my partners know which horses I have. They're going to keep track of what I'm doing, and I'm going to keep track of what they're doing. A guy says he'll take the four. We know we got two horses running now. He's got that horse, I've got this horse. Boom. I see the motion at the six, so I've got the six. I have my stopwatch. I never clear my watch. Boom. I hit my split on my watch. I write that down. I make a visual note. I got a chestnut horse with blinkers, rider in orange, anything I can pick out. I'll make a mental note and I'll put down my split and I'll write six by it. Okay. Now I'll know my watch started on the horse that left the five and my partner's got the horse that left the four. He's on the head now, which means he's in the lane. He's coming at us now. I'm in the middle of the turn five-sixteenths with my five. My six is now over at the half-mile pole. Boom. Now another horse drops in on me at the two. We've got a horse going three-eighths of a mile from the two, which means he's going from the quarter pole and he's going to work out to the seven. He drops in between my partner's half-mile and in front of my five-eighths. I click on it, split, check it. I got a green silk, whatever, I make my mental note. Now I've got three horses running on one watch. Okay. Boom. The starting gate leaves, and I've all of a sudden got four horses breaking from the gate, working that way. Now it gets confusing because you're looking at the gate head on, so you can't really hit your watch to start when they break because Thoroughbreds get two jumps, about ten yards out of the gate before the timer starts. The pole sets out from the gate and looking from where we are at the wire you can't judge that. So we'll wait and let those horses go until they get to the three-sixteenths pole, then we'll start our watches and use a universal number. We know we're going to have seven seconds, all right. Now the first horse that's going to finish is my five because my green silk left the two, he's hitting the wire first but he's going to the seven-eighths pole to work his three-eighths. My five comes to the wire, I hit that, I've got a time on that horse that left the five-eighths. I got a blue helmet on the five. Boom. I've got a tab writer. I'll give him that time, and I'll jot it down. The next one that finishes is my green silk. I see my partner's horse coming to the wire but I know that's his horse, he's got that covered. My green silk goes out to the seven. I'll tell my tab writer that time, and I'll write that number down with the split time that that horse left the two from. Okay, now I've got that. Now I've got my gaters going onto the backstretch. When they come by I'll call out, "I've got four horses from the gate." I've got one FG, which means From Gate, which means he jumped but he didn't work out farther than a quarter of a mile, which doesn't count. I've got two blues and an orange. We don't have any calls from the gate but they have to identify and give the starter the name at the gate when they break. That's the rule. The starter won't break them, ring the bell on them unless they get a name on a horse. So later we'll get a rundown of all the horses that broke from the gate from the starter. We'll tag these horses later on.

So what's happened is that in less than a minute and a half I've just clocked seven horses on one stopwatch, and identified them all. We i.d.'ed them all, and they all got times, correct times. We've rock and rolled a little bit. Anybody can clock one horse from here to there when that's all you got to do. But when you got horses moving in all directions and coming at you from all different places, now we'll find out if you can get yourself organized and tag them all, know who you've got, where they came from. And then when you get done you'll unravel all your splits. You'll figure out all your times.

LAFE BASSETT

Trainers are reluctant to work horses in the rain. They'll put it off if they think it's going to clear up in a couple of days. Not only could there be injuries but then they've got to work outside the dogs, markers that are put out in the middle part of the track, away from the rail, forcing the horses to work wide so as not to further damage the lanes where they regularly run. And, of course, times are going to be slower.

When clocking gets complicated is usually after the twenty-minute break. From 8:20 to 8:40 we'll get eighty percent of our work. If we clock a hundred horses a day, seventy-five of them will work within that first twenty minutes after the break. The reason for this is that the horsemen want to come out when the sun's up, they can see more easily, and it's after the tractors have turned the soil over so the horses can run on a fresh surface.

When a horse comes down to the sixteenth pole and the rider stands up, I don't record nothing, because I think the horse took a bad step. It's entirely up to me to decide whether or not a work is legitimate. For example, one day we had a black letter work by a horse, the fastest work of the day, it was in the mud in fact, a horse crossed that wire and broke both front legs. He was on his knees, and he was dead. The horse was dead. I could record that work, and as a matter of fact, I did. He finished, he finished that work. But if the rider stands up at the sixteenth pole, and the horse bobbles a little bit, and it still crosses the wire in recordable time, I will not use that because that's deceiving to the public. The rider held him up. Our main concern here is to protect the public, to protect them from making bad wagers on unsound horses.

The two major concerns I have as a head clocker are for the public to get an honest shot; and second of all I'm responsible to the investors. The guys that are out here that pay twelve or fifteen million dollars for a baby. That investment is not worth a quarter unless people come out to the races. The owners don't want to hear about phony works, or that a jock pulled up a horse, fixed a race. The owners don't want bad publicity because that ruins their business, ruins their investment. They're the first ones that want you to do an honest job. So my job is seeing that the public is being protected, and that the owners and the gamblers get an honest time. The real good handicappers don't want to hear about how some rider slowed a horse down; that pisses them off because now they can't use their abilities to come up with a winner.

Now mistakes do happen, it's just human error. Numerous times I've gone to take a split on another horse and erroneously cleared my watch. Whoops, I lost those times! So what I'll do is go to the trainer and say, Look, we'll take your time. I don't want him to be penalized because we missed his work. Maybe that horse hasn't raced in a while and needs this work to be eligible again. We have to give him the benefit of the doubt. You have to be fair to the trainer and the owner. Sometimes a bunch of trainers will be hanging out at the rail down by the Gap, where the horses go on and off the racetrack on the backside, and a trainer won't give a call, won't tell the Gap man that his horse is going to work. I might question him about that, ask my Gap clocker to ask him why he worked this horse without giving a call, and he'll say, "Well, these other trainers were standing right there and this is a claiming horse, and I didn't want them to know how fast the horse worked because they might claim him." If that trainer is in the habit of giving me a call most all the time, I'll say thank you very much, it's okay, it's justifiable.

I give anybody the benefit of the doubt until they try to cheat on me. Clocking crews at various tracks have been notorious for being ridden with chicanery, incompetence and ineptitude. I picked my crew myself, and it's been a hard process, a constant battle, day in and day out. I was going to the stewards three times a day with complaints about trainers trying to cheat. I had guys threaten my life. But now this is the best system there is, a great system.

JOE SHUFELT

GAP CLOCKER

My job as Gap man is to take calls from the trainers and feed them via intercom to the clockers upstairs. As I feed them to the clockers, the clockers find the horses, give me the times back, and I give those times to the trainers. My key purpose other than that is to identify the horses properly, to make sure the horse out on the track is the one the trainer says it is. That's just to keep it honest. You've got to let the trainers know you're going to keep it on the level, do it a few times and they won't think any more about lying to you. They'll just go ahead and train their horses.

See, sometimes a horse might be going a little bad, he might be sore and possibly shouldn't race, but the trainer will go ahead and try to run him anyway. He'll drop him down in class, in a claiming race, drop him down cheap enough to where somebody else might be tempted to claim him. But if he can't train, he can't race, that's the rule. A horse must have a recorded work every thirty days to stay eligible to race. So sometimes a man will slide a horse in, a horse that looks comparable but is not the correct horse. He'll try to get that work by in order to keep his other horse eligible so that another trainer or owner might go ahead and claim the sore horse, taking him off your hands. You've cheated the claiming trainer by pawning off a bad, dead horse on him. Also, when the new owner runs the claimed horse, the jockey will think that he's fit and ride him accordingly, and if the horse breaks down on the racetrack, that jock can get hurt. It's important to keep this straight.

I guess I'm still pretty idealistic about all this. As far as I was concerned, when I was thirteen years old, Walter Farley wrote *The Black Stallion* about *me*, that was *my* story and the story of every other thirteen-year-old kid who rode racehorses or wanted to. That's all I ever wanted to do was ride horses. I got too big to do that, but I stayed in the game. Of course, what we're all here for is to find a horse to bet on, that's what everybody is at the racetrack for. This is the only business I know where a man or woman could be poor today and famous tomorrow just because of a horse. If he's a nice horse everybody wants him. The racing secretary wants him, you've got stud horse possibilities, plus the betting.

LAFE BASSETT

I recently had a horse working in the dark, and it was difficult to see the horse break. The horse broke without a call, we did not know the horse was going to work, but we observed the horse breaking and got him from where he started. I wasn't clocking this particular horse, one of my co-workers was, and when the horse came into the stretch I observed him casually, not in detail, because it wasn't one of the horses I was clocking. I did notice a couple of distinguishing marks on him though, and when the horse crossed the wire my co-worker said that he had this horse going a half-mile at :45 ⅘, which is a fast time. As the horse proceeded to the seven-eighths pole I told my Gap man, my spotter, to get the markings on this horse, and I asked him if he had a call from the trainer.

When the Gap man confronted the assistant to the trainer, who was down on the rail watching the work, the assistant gave my man a name that didn't jibe. They gave a bad name, the name of a horse that definitely was not the horse I saw work the fast time. So I made the Gap man call the trainer and ask again. Again the assistant gave us the bad name. I immediately turned the matter over to the Board of Stewards, who are the final arbiters in situations of this nature. The stewards called in the trainer and told him to get in touch with me immediately and to properly identify the horse in question. The trainer sent me word that the horse he'd worked was the one he'd identified to the Gap man. I knew he was lying, because word had gotten to me through another source that this trainer was working two horses that were physically similar, and he persisted in giving us the wrong name. In this case one horse was red and the other was brown, and they both had white left hind feet; but I had seen that the horse that worked also had a white right hind and a small star on his forehead. So he was trying to switch horses on us.

Three days later I went down to the backside and personally confronted the trainer, so that I could hear it straight from his mouth. He gave me the bad name. So I went and recorded the bad name, knowing it was wrong. Now what happens is I have to make sure that that horse that's getting the *bad* work, the other one, that the trainer did not name, does not run; if he runs and I don't catch him, the public is going to be deceived. Well, I kept checking but I never saw the horse work. I don't spot the horse until I see him one afternoon in the winner's circle! The trainer won a race with him!

I immediately called the Board of Stewards and the following morning the trainer was made to appear in front of us. The trainer, of course, denied that he'd improperly identified the horse. This is a very difficult charge to prove, so what we fined him for was his failure to identify the horse prior to its working. It's very tough to prove this kind of thing unless you run up to the horse right after he's worked and check the tattoo on his upper lip, which is how all racehorses are marked with their number. The penalty was the maximum I could levy at that time, and the trainer knew it would be damn tough to get it by me again. This was the first time in my career that a trainer got to the winner's circle on me. We also, by the way, asked the jockey, who'd ridden the horse in the morning work, to identify that horse, and he gave us the bad name, too. As, of course, the assistant trainer did. There's no way that jock didn't know which horse it was because he rides both horses for that trainer. But they both work for the trainer and it's not their responsibility; it's the trainer's. The jock just says, If that's the one the trainer says I worked, then that's the one it was.

Numerous times I've had trainers ask me to look the other way, to go have a cup of coffee at a particular time of the morning. They'll ask me what's my day off. They're just looking for an edge.

There was a head clocker at Golden Gate Fields a few years back, and this is a matter of public record, who phonied up a work for a trainer. The trainer came to him and told him he wanted to enter his horse in a race and didn't have enough workouts to qualify. So this clocker gave the horse a workout, registered it that day. He gave the horse a work of five-eighths of a mile in 1:02 because that was the required distance the horse would have had to go. The horse wasn't even on the grounds; he didn't come on the grounds until two days later. The stewards found out about it, and the clocker was given a $1,500 fine and put on probation for three years.

The easiest part of the clocking process is the actual physical aspect of timing animals running on a stopwatch. The difficulty lies in deciphering who you just timed and timing numerous horses at one time. Hidden or "fictitious" workouts have long been a bane to competent clocking and officiating. Like the crooked jockey, the unscrupulous clocker conjures up the image of a red-faced, cigar-chomping tout, the old-timer with a fedora tilted over one eye and pari-mutuel tickets stuck in the hatband. It's an image that's hard to erase. Touting, of course, is selling information for gain or profit, not unlike the insider-trading scandals that have rocked Wall Street. Because of this unsavory image, and to guard against temptation and noncompliance, we enforce a policy whereby the clockers are not allowed to attend the races.

The racetrack and the stock market are really not that different. Both involve investments in large corporations and their product. We're here to insure the investor that he is getting a fair shot at a return on his money. The large investors are the first to support what we try to achieve. The big owners like Sangster, Gaines, Galbreath, Mellon, all have too much invested in this business to want anything but honesty. It's the small-time, get-rich-quick-no-matter-the-cost types that we have to guard against. And the pressures come from a variety of persons, many of whom invest in the tracks themselves and think of it only in terms of the profits they can reap today, with no thought of the business itself, its heritage or future.

There are those at the racetrack who would be delighted to see me move on, to take my attitude elsewhere. But the good trainers and owners don't require any help. They can make it all right without the crooked clocker, no matter what the conditions are. As long as honesty and integrity are an asset to this industry my position is secure. But I never fool myself; there are a myriad of honest and efficient people in the unemployment lines. People better than I have faced injustice, fought the powers that be and lost. The bottom line for me, though, is that I have to shave every morning, I have to look in the mirror, and I want to know whose eyes are staring back.

The following is a sample of clocker notation by which a horse can be identified.

80 CG Duke of Jandy
$*R_{nst}^{bet}NR\ LF\ u^iA\ LHC^iuTA$

Translation: Born 1980, Chestnut Gelding named Duke of Jandy. Star to the right with a narrow strip between nostrils to the right—left front under inside ankle—left hind coronet—inside under tendon ankle.

MAX "THE PRINCE" MILANO

The tricky part about the works is that they don't say that this horse was driven into the ground and overmedicated and that same amount of medication would not be legal in the afternoon. What it doesn't say is that this horse has been absolutely pushed to the maximum. If a horse works five-eighths of a mile in a minute, or the horse works in fifty-eight seconds, hey, that looks like a great work. But that horse may never be able to run that fast in a race. And that horse that won the training race on Saturday morning just outran seven horses that will not make it to the races. You know, when you work an old horse in a minute, a proven racehorse, it's a lot different than when you work seven pieces of shit in a minute.

W NELS HOEL

TELETYPE OPERATOR FOR THE
DAILY RACING FORM

e keep track of all the works the horses run in the morning and break 'em down into distances and times. I get them to the *Racing Form* real quick because a lot of the horses might be racin' in the next day or two. We gotta get these times in the *Form* so the public will have it. The *Form* is published in both Los Angeles and New Jersey. We'll call in with condition rundowns and entries for the races two days ahead. There are two *Form* editions for each day, the blow-off and the main edition. The blow-off is really the proof edition, the one that the racing office and other people can make changes on and fix for the regular edition. Like, today is Friday, so we're gonna take entries for Tuesday, and tomorrow morning we'll have a blow-off for Tuesday's paper.

The clockers run off their own sheet of the day's works and give them to us, then I get them to the *Form*. We also provide information on each individual race. We have a crew of three, and one guy calls the race as it happens and another writes it all down in his shorthand. The caller isolates each horse, says who broke on top and all that. When they get a quarter of a mile he calls them again, with margins, the distances between them. All through the race. The person who takes it down will then break it down further, noting that the one horse was seventh, eighth, seventh by six lengths behind the leader, seventh by five, and so on. We have the odds of the races, any overweights, jockey changes, handle, payoffs, times of the races, breeding of the winner, everything. When the transcription of the race is finished and all of the information is complete, I send it out to the *Form*. Each race will carry a description, too, a complete synopsis. This entire process takes about ten minutes after a race is over. Ten minutes later, bam! LA's got it. The crew has to be quick and accurate because they're not gonna run that race over again for you. We're pretty good. We're a good team, I think.

Parsing the charts in the *Daily Racing Form* is a fascinating exercise. Each chart does, in fact, embody the "story" of a race, just as the box score of a baseball game tells its own tale. The following code of abbreviations is used by the *Form* to identify the sex and age of the various participants: "c"=colt (an entire male through four years of age); "h"=horse (an entire male five years old or older); "g"=gelding (a male horse who has been unsexed); "f"=filly (a female through four years of age); "m"=mare (a female five years old or older); and "rig"=ridgling (a half-castrated male horse or a horse with one or both organs of reproduction absent from the sac). Information used by permission of *Daily Racing Form,* Inc.

LEON LEWIS
STEWARD

There are three stewards assigned at each racetrack. We convene at about eight in the morning. Our duties are really the toughest because we have all kinds of cases. We review films of the races and decide whether or not foul claims are legitimate; we hear the cases of riders who have been called in for infractions; we hear medical violation cases. We watch the running of the races and make certain that everything has proceeded properly.

I worked my way up over the years through the ranks. I rode for three years, worked in the parking lot, worked the scales, as a steward's aide; so I know the entire operation. In a race, when we put up the inquiry sign, we think there's grounds for disqualification. An owner, a jockey, a trainer with a horse in the race, can also claim a foul if they desire. We have four cameras on the racetrack, including two head-on cameras. We look at every angle that we can to determine if an infraction has occurred. If we feel that a horse was interfered with to the point that it cost another a better placing, then we'll disqualify the horse and rider responsible and place that horse behind the horse interfered with.

The toughest ones, I think, are those leaving the starting gate. Jockeys don't have as much control or restraint on a horse leaving the gate as they do after a few strides out; they have to give them enough rein so the horse will break, and when a horse breaks a little off-stride or something, he might go in or out. You don't see too many disqualifications leaving the starting gate just because the horses are more difficult to control at that point.

If we decide to suspend a rider for a few days, he can appeal our decision to the state horseracing board. The board will hear the case and can stay our ruling. If the jockey loses his appeal, he can take his case to the courts, to the judicial system, if he so chooses.

Once the race is made official for betting purposes nothing can be changed so far as the pari-mutuel wagering is concerned. The payoff remains. But as far as the placing of horses, it could be. The horse might be disqualified from the purse money, but the betting public is not affected.

We also have to approve any transfer of ownerships. Each owner's financial obligations have to be met and settled before we'll approve a transfer. We also approve every licensee at the racetrack, from general manager to carpenter. The racetrack is very different than any other business. It's a little world of its own. There are some people who never go outside the boundaries of the track unless they're shipped to another meeting. They get in a van and ride out with their horses.

We keep a daily record of our activities, we keep minutes of our meetings and send reports to the commissioner of the state racing board. But mostly our duties have to do with dealing with riding situations. If a jockey permits his horse to duck out into another horse, knocks him off-stride, we handle the situation. We have to approve new riders; they have to convince us they're ready to ride. It really takes years to become a rider; it's not something you learn overnight. The sense of pace, how to place your horse—your reactions have to be just snap. I mean they have to be right there. You can't hesitate and think about it, because if you do you might pick yourself up off the ground.

JAY D. HOOP, D.V.M.
OFFICIAL VETERINARIAN

We average about a hundred horses a day that we have to check. We have to find out whether they're bleeders or not, if blood gets into their lungs when they run, and we have to make certain those horses get treated. We inspect all the horses that are running in a day; they get a thorough examination each time they run, and they must be sound throughout. If a trainer feels that his horse that's already scheduled to go can't run that day, then we go and check him out. If the horse is sick, has colic, abdominal pain, say, we scratch him from the race, and he goes on the vet's list. If he's sore or lame, we'll require that he be worked before we'll allow him to run. We test blood to ensure that medication is used within the limits we've established.

They don't allow the use of medication in New York, but in California we feel that if a horse bleeds he should have something to take care of it. In New York they feel if a horse bleeds then he's defective, flawed, and if the trainer can't figure out a way to keep the horse running without bleeding, then he has to take him out of the New York jurisdiction and run him where they allow the use of Lasix. Lasix is a furosemide, a diuretic that takes fluids out of the body. When you take fluids out of the body, you're taking out potential problems that constrict the vessels. The Lasix also reduces the blood pressure; it's a common treatment for people with heart problems, too. Horses during exertion hemorrhage in their lungs, and the blood comes up their trachea and out their nose. Many times, however, the majority of times, the blood will not show up unless you scope them, run a tube down their nostrils into the trachea. A horse has to bleed very badly for it to come out the nose.

A trainer can try to draw a horse rather than give him Lasix. He can take the feed away, and all the fluids. This is so the horse doesn't have the digestive process going on at the same time he's running. When the blood is forced through a vessel and there's too much pressure, it ruptures. Lasix removes the fluids from all the tissues, not just in the one area. In so doing, it removes potassium from the body, and potassium is a very necessary part of the nutrition and health of the body, so that potassium must be replaced. If the horse is on a continual Lasix treatment, then electrolytes are given back to the horse because they contain potassium. In New York they allow use of bioflabinoids, citrus pulp, peelings of oranges and lemons, as a treatment for bleeding. They also use gelatins. If those don't work, they just abandon the horse, send him someplace else where he can be treated with Lasix. As I say, we examine the horses endoscopically, with a very bright light clear down into the trachea and into some of the bronchials. We know if the horse has bled. Each time the horse runs he has to be treated with Lasix three hours before the race. The horse is put into a detention stall and separated from the others so that the vet who goes into the barn will know who the Lasix horse is, and he won't allow the horse any other medication; we don't want the trainer to give the horse any other medication that might help him run better and that might be covered up by the Lasix. It's to prevent any tampering with the horse.

RICHARD SOMERS

The first time a horse gets Lasix it definitely skims him. It'll definitely send a horse the first time he's on it, boost his performance. It helps any kind of a horse, good or mediocre. A "Bleeder's

List" is posted at the racetrack so that everyone can know what horses have been treated. But then it has a negative effect on them the longer they're on it. Like anybody that's on any kind of diuretic, it takes strength out of you, burns up B vitamins, a lot of potassium. Not only do you have to keep the horse on potassium if he's on Lasix, but also on water absorption because they're losing so much. In the end, though, Lasix will burn a horse out.

JAY D. HOOP, D.V.M.

I also appear before the stewards whenever there's a complaint regarding medications. Perhaps there's been an overage of a certain drug, or use of drugs that do not appear in the permission book—anything against regulations. A horse might have been treated with sulfa along with antibiotics if he's got a cough or a cold. The trainer runs him, and in the random testing following the race the sulfa shows up. The state requires that a complaint be issued against the trainer for using sulfa, and the stewards either penalize him by fine or suspend him, or both. It depends what his record is.

I have to check the horses out before the race, when they're brought over to the receiving barn before going to the paddock. That's how it's done in California. The horses get checked over twice, in their own barn and in the receiving barn. You don't want to let a lame horse go over to the racetrack because when the jockey gets on him, that's a hundred plus pounds on his back and he could buckle, really be hurt. The horse will jog around the track after leaving the paddock, and if the jockey's not satisfied with the way the horse is going he'll bring him over to the track veterinarian and have him checked again. If the vet feels the horse shouldn't go, he'll contact the stewards and recommend the horse be scratched right there at the starting gate. If that happens, whoever's bet on that horse automatically has their wager transferred to the favorite on the board. They still have a bet.

After each race we'll test certain horses for drugs, a urine test. If it's an exacta race, where you can make a bet on the first two finishers, we'll test both the first and second horses. If it's not an exacta race, then we'll take only the winner plus the leading favorite, if another horse was the favorite. Then we take a random horse, so the trainers don't know whether their horse will be tested or not. Each day we run about thirty to thirty-five post-race tests. We bring these horses into the veterinarian's barn, bathe them, give them alcohol, just as if they were back in their own barn, walk them around and cool them out. After twenty or thirty minutes we take the blood and urine. It might take us three or four hours to get the urine, and the horses are under strict surveillance all the time. We check the lip tattoos to make sure it's the correct horse. We check the tendons. We make sure the horse is properly licensed. If he checks out, then he's returned to the trainer. The trainer or his assistant, his representative, must sign an affidavit saying he witnessed the procedure, so we have legal evidence of what's transpired.

If a horse goes down on the racetrack, goes over the rail or something, there's a track veterinarian that treats him. If the horse is gone, both legs hopelessly broken, say, then the horse can be put down on the track. If we can get him into the ambulance, then we bring him back to our barn and let the trainer's own vet look at him. There are about fourteen veterinarians who work for the various trainers on the racetrack. We take a blood test so we can determine the horse's condition at the time of the fall. If the horse is put down, we require the trainer's veterinarian to provide us with a postmortem report.

The saddest situation is when a horse has to be euthanized on the track. It's traumatic for the trainer, the public, the vet. You do what you can to prevent it in every way possible. Some horses get upset by crowd noise, they'll get spooked and go right through the rail. A horse named Gate Dancer used to get so unnerved by the noise that he wore blinkers, had cotton stuffed in his ears and a kind of hood over his hears, all one unit, to keep him calm, shut out the crowd. The paddock judge has to approve the use of all special equipment: bandages, bits, shoes, blinkers. The trainer must notify the paddock judge in advance, before he brings that horse over to the racetrack, if he intends to change any gear. When the trainer enters the horse, he must list the equipment that horse will be wearing, and the paddock judge has that information to check against when he's brought over. We try to cover everything.

MAX "THE PRINCE" MILANO

You ask a doctor to fix a horse and he does whatever he does and says, yeah, the horse is fixed. So in theory the animal is fixed. But the real question is, can he race again? That's the variable. The throat operation was successful, but can he race? Most vets have no racing experience so their out is, I fixed him, I corrected the problem, but it doesn't help him race.

I had a horse that had a wind problem, and we had his throat operated on twice, cost me thousands each time. I got the horse back and got on him and asked him to step a half-mile. After an eighth of a mile his head popped up and I decided that this horse is not fixed. I called the veterinarian and he told me to send him back. Bang, it cost me another fifteen hundred. Soon thereafter I was reading a horsemen's journal and I read about this same problem. The article said that although surgery is often indicated, it's rarely successful. So, if I'd had a sharp veterinarian in the beginning, he would have said this and I could have saved the money and got rid of the horse. Instead, the horse was in training from May to October at twelve hundred dollars a month plus all medical assistance, which means you chase it with another eight to ten thousand. This comes under the heading of experience. If you're fifty years old and you make that mistake, you're stupid; if you're twenty years old, you're learning.

My experience with veterinarians is that if you need a doctor you're in trouble. The vet comes in and he sits there for exactly thirty seconds and he's gone. He's got anywhere from ten to twenty other clients on the racetrack, he's got other horses to treat. He's got a lot on his mind, he's preoccupied, like anybody else. He walks up to a tendon, a knee, and usually what he says is, "Don't worry." The reason he says this is because if something goes really wrong with the horse you'll have to call him and you have to pay him to do the work on it. So why should he ever worry? He's not worried. It's not his problem.

In 1960 a vet came to the barn, he wormed the occasional horse, took care of the odd problem, and went on his way. Nowadays nothing moves without a veterinarian. It costs you a hundred dollars a whack to run a horse with all the different types of medications, legal medications, synthetic products that they feel enhances the horse's ability to express himself. Of course, the horse can't talk, so he can't tell the vet he don't need or want this stuff. The owner is in another city, the trainer is sitting in the kitchen drinking coffee, and the vet is in the barn. The horse is in his hands.

Of course it's terribly obvious that if a horse just broke his leg then the vet gives him a shot for the pain. That's fine. Hey, doc, this horse is in tomorrow, can you give him a shot of Bute—Butazolidin, an anti-inflammatory drug legal in California—that's cool. Hey, doc, this is a Lasix horse, can you treat him for a bleeder. Okay. You have to keep in mind that a horse operates off of two nervous systems, the motor nerve and the sensory nerve, so there are situations where you can do something about taking away pain from either of the nerves, but not both; to take away pain from both of the nerves would incapacitate the animal. The vets very often do not really understand about keeping the horses in racing condition.

In the 1960s and '70s people got away with murder insofar as the use of drugs was concerned. They test more now but the urine and blood tests cannot test for everything, cannot test for every kind of medication there is; so it's like what's hot and what's not. There are people who do that, who don't know how to bring a horse around without drugs, who are impatient. And with some new vet, twenty-five years old, fresh out of school, with no practical experience whatsoever, not having been around the racetrack before, he has no concept of what works and what doesn't. He gives an opinion to an inexperienced owner, the foolish trainer, and they take it. This confuses me because I don't know how they can assume the doc's opinion is valid if that guy just walked on the backside. If you take a vet who's sixty or seventy years old, who's got a ton of experience, raced in the '50s, the '60s, the '70s, well, all right. The racetrack is a game of experience.

In my experience I've found it's best to avoid contact with veterinarians. I try to evaluate the problem myself. I get on the horse and if an ankle feels bad I check on it. I've never seen an ankle like this, I don't know how this one is going to work because I've never seen problem ankles like this work out; so I don't deal with it, I pass it on to another person who is maybe a little more creative in that department, has more experience or insight. But it's also been my experience that if a horse doesn't run for me, he doesn't run for anybody. If a horse can't get by me then he can't run. I don't need the vet or the stewards to tell me that. I'm my own steward in that I know the rules and I know what works. I don't try to make a silk purse out of a sow's ear, and I don't try to fantasize or create an illusion about what's in front of me. So I don't come into contact very often with the officials.

Some veterinarians, if you turn them loose, will assume the bills are just being paid by an insurance company and take off. Some of them are so unrealistic about the expectation it's wild, and they act too fast. You should do absolutely nothing to try to fix a horse until you know exactly what's wrong and what the proper procedure should be. Too many vets are too quick on the trigger, and that's from inexperience. It might be better to go slow, stick the horse's legs in some ice for a few days, back off and wait. I mean, horses have obvious physical handicaps because they're being made to run fast. Veterinarians have to understand that there often is really nothing they can do to help this horse run.

The racetrack is one place where the longer you're around the better you'll do. Theoretically, at least. It takes time to know what to do and what not to do. You're not at your best when you're young. It's a constant learning experience, for trainers and veterinarians alike.

PAUL FISHER
HORSE IDENTIFIER

I'm in at six-thirty every day and go to the racing office and check the certificates on the horses that are scheduled to run. Horses that are nonstarters before in this state we got to tattoo, to brand 'em. We attempt to do it the day before they race. About eight-thirty I start goin' to the various barns and make sure the horses that are goin' to race are the right horses. I check 'em later by the receiving barn when they're brought over before the race and it better be the same horse or it's adios, he's scratched immediately. We'll then attempt to find out who that horse really is, which is no problem, really. Sometimes, when the horse got shipped in, the hauler took the wrong horse. It's a very honest mistake ninety-nine percent of the time. I've got pictures of every horse, their tattoo number; it's hard to get one by me.

I've been with horses all my life, ever since I was a child in Colorado. I was in the Mule Pack in the army, went into the veterinary service, worked as a groom and horse trainer. After I got out of the service I happened to step on the right corner and a man from the Thoroughbred Racing Protective Bureau hired me. I was sent to Oaklawn Park in Hot Springs, Arkansas, first; learned the tattoo system and about the policing agency of the racetracks. I traveled all over the country, to all the racetracks: from Hot Springs to Phoenix, Memphis, Keeneland, Churchill Downs, Cincinnati, Denver, Omaha, Seattle, back down South, New York. People on the racetrack know who I am. Thirty years now in this place. If they don't know me, they'd better, or they'll get a rude awakening. I'm a mean bastard!

RICHARD SOMERS
PRICEMAKER

I make up the betting line that is published in the racing program. I take about twenty minutes to handicap each race, and it's a lot of concentrated effort, taking in what's on paper, adding in your own opinions, and then taking it to the abstract effect. A line must balance. You're going to distribute one hundred percent of the money back to the public at the end of the race, plus you're going to have a track takeout that's running about twenty-three percent now. So that means I've got 123 percent to work with. I have to equate my odds with that overall total. If I've got a horse laying two to one, then that accounts for thirty-three points; if I lay him four to one, that's twenty points, and so on. In other words, two to one is a total of three; I divide one hundred by three, and that equals thirty-three percent. Four to one comes to twenty percent.

I set up a guideline and take into consideration the breakage, the rounding off of the payoff to the nearest dime. If it comes out to a certain figure, there is money that's not paid out, and that money goes to the racetrack and the state. With fewer horses in a race, short fields, there's less breakage, so I try to make my total come out between 118 and 122 points. For a larger field, say a ten- to twelve-horse field, I'll try to make it work somewhere between 122 and 126 points.

If I see a horse that I figure will at race time go off at six to five, a favorite, I'll usually lay that horse eight to five and let the public carry him down to six to five. I don't like to lay a horse eight to five when I think he's going to go to two to one; I'd rather let the betting public carry him down. I want to be real close on my favorite, the chalk, and on my last horse, because if I'm not, I've got no chance in between.

W LAFE BASSETT

When the horse is the favorite he's called the chalk. That's an expression that comes from the old gambling days where a chalkboard was used, and the odds on the favorites were changing all the time. A horse that was being bet all the time, that was a hot commodity, got a piece of chalk left under his name on the board because he got so much action, so he was called the chalk.

H RICHARD SOMERS

Here's a race that will be the seventh race on the card. I work off the *Racing Form* charts most of the time, when it's available, and I look for connections in it, that people bet on. One of the things I'll always notice is the odds the horse went off at the last time it ran. In this race I see a horse moving in from Santa Anita and he's going to get a top jock. I see that this horse is coming out of a barn that does not win a lot of races, not a barn the public cares for very much; they don't respect the trainer. But they are going to pick up that a top jockey will be riding the horse and the horse is coming from a top racetrack, so they'll give credence to that. The horse has been running against good horses but hasn't been faring well. He's seventy to one on the grass but that day they ran him way over his head, above his conditions, and he didn't like the grass. His race before that was more in line with his conditions, his quality, and he was bet down to nine to one that time. It was a route race, a long race, and to me it looks as if he's more of a sprinter. He's got some decent workout times.

I run down each horse this way and compare all of the horses in the race, taking into consideration every possibility, and I assume the horses are all fit to run. As it turns out, I'll make that horse that's coming in from Santa Anita seven to two, my second favorite in the race, because I think he fits very well with the horses he's got to run against. I think this is a good spot for him.

After the race.

As it turned out, the public bet the horse at five to one; they didn't like him as much as I thought they would, and raised the odds. He ran to his Santa Anita form, a race typical to that form, which is not good. The public usually overbets a horse from Santa Anita because they tend to think those horses are much better than those from lesser racetracks, and they aren't necessarily better. Even though he was only five to one, he was still overbet according to his form. This was a six-horse field, and he finished next to last.

I remember one perfect line I had that came in a very obscure race, in a real bad spot in the card. It was a maiden twelve-five, all nonwinners running in a cheap race, and all the horses were just total bunks; slow, slower and slowest. Every call at every pole was double digits. Twelfth by eleven lengths, tenth by fourteen lengths. Every one was like that. The horses in the race that hadn't started had real obscure workout patterns, had no talent showing in any performance. There was nothing that I could clue in on. There were no especially good trainer-jockey combinations, things that mean money is going to show. Anyway, the line came up just like I said it would, and I got great reviews for that. Even one of the stewards said something to me about it. One of the guys asked me how I'd done it, seeing as how there was so little tangible information to go on. I just told him that I do each race the same way. The key is that I have to be real close on my favorite.

JOHN GIBSON
TRACK ANNOUNCER

My mom used to take me to the track when I was a little kid. At first I didn't care much, wasn't really interested in the races, but then eventually I started paying attention. Somebody gives you a couple of bucks and you bet it to show on some horse, he scores, and that's it. Once a winner you think, hey, this is where it's at, this is better than going down to the playground.

It got so I really liked the races and when I got out of college I bought a couple of harness horses. I became a harness driver, and I trained. I didn't stay in the harness game too long, though. Harness racing doesn't have a very good reputation so far as being honest goes, and justifiably so, in my opinion. But even when I was in high school I was interested in being the track announcer. I thought it'd be a terrific profession. I was always in all the plays in school. I had a theatrical side. I was more of a cut-up, the jackass, to tell the truth. Combine that with horseracing, and here I am.

When I was working around the racetrack, to make the time pass more easily I'd pretend I was calling the races. I was working for a man who was good friends with the announcer, and he tape recorded me one day when I didn't know it. He played the tape for the regular announcer, and I wound up calling qualifying races. I remember when I first did it I was so damn nervous I couldn't even hold my binoculars. Finally I got more and more comfortable, and one day I got a write-up in the newspaper. It said, ". . . and the races were expertly called by a young, upcoming announcer named John Gibson." So the track started letting me call the last regular race every night. I got a great response, and the steady announcer took offense. Only natural, I guess, but there I was; I was on my way.

I haven't got the kind of ego where I need to be stroked constantly. I know when I do a good job, and when I do a bad job. But the people down below who are winning and losing have another perspective. You can give the losers the best call of a race in the world, but if their horse didn't make it, you're an asshole. If you give the winners the worst call in the world, well, their horse made it, so you're the greatest. The people who win kind of relive their score with my voice saying so-and-so up front, so-and-so getting up. You touch everybody down there eventually. I was twenty-five when I started announcing Thoroughbred races. That's ten years ago.

I classify myself as an entertainer, calling the races and giving good information and trying to make it exciting. The man I idolized as an announcer was Harry Hansen, who was the track announcer at Hollywood Park. When I worked there I would go up to his booth every day and visit with him. He was the ultimate announcer, dead serious about everything he did. He was greatly respected by the fans because he was never hokey, he was always very straightforward in his approach. He fit Hollywood Park perfectly. He might have seemed to some like an unspectacular announcer, speaking in a monotone, but he took a classic approach and gained the fans' respect. Harry was respectful toward them, and they returned it. He was an absolute professional.

You have to be descriptive in calling a race, but most of all you have to be accurate. I know the colors of the silks, who's running the horses, the riders. I do my homework for the races so I'll be accurate. But the truth is that this job is actually very boring. Very, very boring. I mean, the horses just get out there and go around the track, and you're calling horses and positions, and after a time it's all the same. I think all jobs at the racetrack are rather boring if you're not wagering. This game is wagering. Not too long ago somebody in management said to the employees that we do not want you to wager, we look down on you if you wager; we're paying you to be there and work. Which is a very true statement. But then an employee stood up and said, "What the hell are we running here, a church? I mean, let's tell the truth, you know, we're running a gambling establishment here." Management has a good point: If you want to gamble at the races, that's nice, just do it on your own time. And I think gambling is a very serious problem at the race-track among employees, more so than management even realizes. On pay day the handle at the track goes up considerably. If I was running the racetrack, and I was the general manager, I would make damn sure that every paycheck was mailed home. But to be honest, to be truly honest, they don't really want it that way. They really, truly don't. They don't want to encourage wagering among employees, but they know what's going on.

I used to bet a lot more than I do now. I don't normally do it at all now. The simple reason is that I call the races better if I don't bet. I used to do both real well, but it's like getting a kiss and getting pinched in the ass at the same time. It hurts but it feels good, so you don't know. I enjoy it, I love to bet, to win, but you can't combine the two.

I used to put everything I had into every race, give the call all my energy every time out of the gate. I used to be completely drained when I left the racetrack. I've had to slow down a little bit. It's like when Willie Nelson's up there on the stage, and he might sing a song if he really feels like singing it; and maybe the next time he sings it it's just a song that he's singing. Maybe that's the way it is with me. I used to say stuff like when they hit the wire and it was real tight, "Whooooooooaaaaaaa!" It was just something I did, something that rolled out. I cut it out, and I don't even know why. I didn't do it intentionally, it just stopped. I didn't really know I used to do so many things. I'd hear the tape of it on the radio, and I couldn't believe it. They were just subconscious. It was amazing. I'd listen to the replays and think, "I said that?"

Everybody makes mistakes, and you've got to know how to cover for yourself. That's how you keep yourself going. I don't care if it's John Gibson at Golden Gate Fields, or Marshall Cassidy at Belmont Park or Jim Byers at Hollywood. Anybody. You're going to make mistakes; you're going to make them all the time. Now you don't want to make a classic mistake, that's the thing. Call the wrong horse in a big race or something like that. I've had a lot of trouble out of that starting gate, for instance. Some horses break and then drop back, and you've called him already. That comes from not actually handicapping the race and looking in there and knowing who's the true speed. I mean if you knew who the true speed was and somebody, an old closer, got away clean, you know he'll run fifty yards and you'll just let him go without a call because you know he's going back to the field; he'll settle into his spot. A speed horse breaks a little flat-footed, he's going to rush up, so you got to be ready for that. And that first hundred yards out of the gate a lot of announcers avoid that problem by just not saying a damn thing until they're clear. I don't like doing that, though; I like something to be said immediately from the gate.

I think the public wants truthfulness out of you. They don't want to be thinking that you're putting them on in any way. But sometimes I actually get upset with the crowd. If I say something and don't get the response I feel I should get from them, I get upset. Sometimes I'll come back with a simpler explanation of my original statement and hopefully they can grasp that, especially when it concerns an inquiry. They might boo, and then the next time we show it back on the replay monitors I might say, "Now ladies and gentlemen, if you watch very closely, you will see this contact being made. Now right here you'll see the horse on the inside come over." In other words, don't give me this crap; I think it was a very justifiable disqualification. I actually always felt the stewards should have their own microphone to explain their own damn inquiries. Why should I be the go-between? They made the decision, let them explain it.

After all this time, there still is not a day that I get up and don't enjoy coming to the racetrack. I enjoy it. I don't know what it is but if I worked at any other job I'd probably be wishing I was at the track. It's just that at times the job gets boring when you're not wagering. I don't think we'd have too many fans out there if we just raced horses without any betting. If that was actually the sport, I don't think you'd draw too many people. The wagering concept is the whole game. I used to be kind of a high-handed person, but I'm not too much like that anymore. I kind of got mellow. You know, do your job and get out of Dodge.

Pierre Oller, a French perfume salesman, invented the concept of mutual wagering, establishing a betting system whereby the actual odds would be based on the ratio of money bet on one horse to what was bet on other horses in the race. This was to circumvent wagering with bookmakers who took an extremely high percentage. Oller took five percent of the total monies bet as his commission, thus assuring a ninety-five percent return to the winning bettors.

JOE SANTOS
PARI-MUTUEL CLERK

I started working as a mutuel clerk in 1959 at Santa Anita, where I was galloping horses in the mornings. Then I had a bad accident, broke my back and pelvis in a fall, and when I came back to the racetrack I still had the clerk's job. Now they have a computer that issues the bets and cashes the tickets, but in the old days it was much harder. If you were at a ten-dollar window and a guy came up and wanted to bet a hundred dollars, you'd have to punch out ten tickets. Now it's just one from any window. And you had to use a pencil to figure out payoffs, and multiply, and you could very easily make a mistake. Now the computer does all the work. Mutuel clerks make over a hundred dollars a day. You're not supposed to have a program or a *Form,* and you're not supposed to bet.

You see all kinds of people at the windows. Everybody has a system, too. You generally see the same people every day, the repeat players, and you can tell without even asking if they're having a good day. You know by the way they approach and what they say. People just have to share what's happening with them. A guy will say, "I'm gonna give up gambling, I just lost my ass." Or they'll cash a ticket for $3,000 and say, "I'm just getting even." I love this job. I've had people come to my window and cash tickets for five or six thousand dollars, someone I've never seen before in my life, and if I don't have the money on hand I'll have to order it. So we'll stand there and chat for a minute or two, and when you pay them off they're really in a good mood and they'll maybe throw you a couple of hundred dollar bills. One day a guy came up after the previous race had been over for about ten minutes and handed me a fifty-dollar bill. I asked him what number he wanted to bet it on, and he said, "No, this is for you." He tells me he came up to my window at the last second, and I punched him out the winning ticket. He said if I hadn't been so fast, he'd never have had the ticket. It was the computer, not me, of course. I said thank you, and I've never seen the guy again. So like I say, it's a really good job.

It's also against the rules for mutuel clerks to tout, of course. But there's nothing in the rules that says if someone wants to give you something you can't take it. As far as touting goes, though, I've been around the racetrack thirty years and I never really made enough money gambling to brag about. I never was a good gambler, and I'm not a good handicapper. If I had to make a living betting on horses, I couldn't do it. That's why I'm working here.

JIMMY RUGGERI
STARTER

I'm responsible for getting the horses in the starting gate and getting 'em out as best as possible. Get 'em out in a line, and to watch out for the riders, that's the main thing. That's what the assistant starters are for, to control the horses. We keep a book on the horses, know the good ones and bad ones. We try to keep one or two men loose to go to horses that are causing trouble. If it goes well and don't have a hold-up, you can get nine head in there and straightened away and out in less than a minute.

I hold the starting gun behind my back because some of the riders are pretty sharp and they'll look for any edge they can get. I'm up in my tower, and I keep it out of sight. You can't leave it out there where they can see your finger. I've been working on the gate for nineteen years, so I know what some of them boys is trying to do.

BOB DUPONT
FORMER ASSISTANT STARTER

Working in the starting gate is a bad place, worse than shoeing. Your job in there is to try to keep the horse straight and get 'em all away even, which rarely happens. The assistant starter stands on a little ledge about six inches wide. You got to have the bridle rein in one hand and maybe the horse's mane in the other, or an ear, and you got to keep your shoulders away so you don't knock the rider off. A lot of horses have to be tailed, too, held by the tail because they'd flip over backward in the gate. Sometimes you wind up down inside underneath that horse. He'll pull you down in there, and you better get out fast.

I got 'em hook their leg up in the overhead part of the gate; rear up and get their leg stuck. They should have been tailed, but if he wasn't, he will be next time, they'll have the book on him. If a horse rears, the rider can fall off behind him and be squeezed in the gate, which is locked, cam locked, and he can easily be killed, crushed to death. After you get the horse in there, once in a while he'll start turning away and you holler, "Whoa, boss, whoa, boss!" so the starter won't take it. If the horse is turned the wrong way, then the rest of them are gone and he's gonna be five or six lengths behind from the start.

When you load the horses in, the guy who leads 'em has got his hand on the ear, and he don't jump up because he'll get the door shut behind him; and as long as he keeps a hold of that ear, we call it the lug, the horse won't kick. And you've got your arm locked with the other guy on the opposite side underneath him, and you load him right in there.

The riders got the worst job in the world because they're on top of a thousand pounds of dynamite. It's got nothing but speed and no brains. Now, they say a horse is smart. Shit, they're not smart. If they were smart, you couldn't get 'em to run out there. Those guys who're on top of those horses got to manage them and it takes a lot of power.

LAFE BASSETT

If a horse is a particularly bad actor in the gate and grabbing the bridle doesn't hold him, the assistant starter will maybe bite on the horse's ear just to get their attention until the break. The favorite always has a starter, too, 'cause they always want to make sure those horses are covered. The riders want to get all the advantage they can get; in the old days when I first started getting on horses you could put your foot up against the side of the gate and feel the clip from the starter's gun, and when that latch went up you'd lunge forward with your horse and off you'd go, and maybe get a little head start. A lot of riders will hold onto the mane, wrap the mane around a finger because some horses break so fast; they're stretching so fast, you better have a hunk of mane so the horse don't just drop out from under you. You want to leave with the horse, not have him leave you.

When you're in the gate on the horse, and the horse goes to do something, maybe rear up, you get out of the stirrups and up on the little shelf off to the side. Sometimes the horse is so high, dancing all day 'cause he knows he's gonna run, and then all of a sudden he's loaded into this two-foot, two-and-a-half-foot wide gate, and where is he going to go? If you're a jock, it's like being locked into a closet with a mad grizzly bear. That's just what it's like. And if you happen to be the guy in the one hole, the first post position, in an eight- or nine-horse field, you got to wait for everyone to load after you. And the horse next to you nine times out of ten will jump, or the rider's foot will hit the side, and your horse thinks it's time to go, and right away that's trouble. One after another the horses hit the sides, and each time the other horses jump.

This is the most dangerous moment for the jocks, the most vulnerable they are to damage. A dozen years ago at Santa Anita a jock named Alvaro Pineda was on a horse in the gate that went down on his face, which brought Pineda up out of the saddle, and then the horse reared up, flinging Pineda up against the arch of the gate, crushing his skull right where his helmet met the back of his neck. That's why they now have cushions on the underside of the the gate arches. The day after Pineda died they had cushions.

It can be absolutely horrifying to be in the gate and all of a sudden the horse goes to his knees and drags you down there with him. You get thrown off and under them and hell, you're going to get trampled to death. The horse has *got* to step on you. I've had them flip over, hung over the back of them and the starter had to pull me out. A horse reared over on me one time. He used his body and pinned me and I couldn't get loose, so the starter ripped me out just before the horse flipped *under* the gate. They had to move the whole gate to get the horse up. And the crazy thing is, that horse won a race the next day.

It's a known fact that you don't complain about starters. I've had horses load in and try to go under the front latch. They're going down and you're standing up, yelling for an assistant starter, and if you're a complainer you just may not get one. You're in such a precarious position, it's so tight, that you don't dare complain. You just grin and bear it. Another thing is, you could bitch about a starter or assistant starter and the next thing you know one of 'em has a hold of your horse's head, just holding him steady, and bang, there they go, and he holds your horse just a bit longer, and you're two lengths behind. So a lot of times you'll find that when a jock walks into a bar and several starters are in there, he'll buy them a round. The starters take care of the jocks, and the jocks better act right to them. These are hard-nosed ex-rodeo hands, most of them, and they're all former riders. These guys are about half-tough, all of 'em. Manhandlers. It takes a lot of guts and strength to jump in and grab a twelve-hundred pound horse that's ready to run. It's a tight spot in there.

THE GRANDSTAND

"Figuration, more commonly called handicapping, is the art of picking winners off the figures, or past performances, which may be interpreted in as divers ways as the entrails of the sacrificial sheep."

—*A.J. Liebling*

I'll never forget the time my friend Big Steve and I lost all of our money at Churchill Downs betting on the Kentucky Derby. For one of the few times in our early years as handicappers (we were seventeen), we'd reckoned on the favorite taking the race, bet everything we had on him, and the animal finished well up the track.

The novelist William Kennedy remembered in an essay an uncle of his, a veteran horseplayer, pointing out to him an obviously down-and-out individual picking up a butt from the gutter, and saying, "There's a guy who used to play the favorites." Kennedy's uncle knew what he was talking about: Big Steve and I got what we deserved.

Big Steve, however, even at that tender age, never missed an opportunity for *le grand geste.* As we departed the racetrack, Steve stopped in front of a blind, crippled man lying on the ground just outside the gate who was selling pencils, which he held in a torn and battered hat, for five cents apiece. Steve reached into his right front pants pocket, turned it inside out and came up with his last nickel. He tossed the coin into the poor guy's crumpled fedora. "Keep the pencil," Steve said.

There is a large gulf between handicapping and betting. An ability to properly analyze a race does not necessarily translate into success as a player. "The trick to handicapping," the groom Sam Bones told me, "is finding a horse that can run easier than he has to, to not have to run as fast as he can to win. It's difficult to find that right situation, but when you do, then it's a good gamble."

W RICHARD SOMERS

PRICEMAKER

ith some people, betting on the horses is a religious experience, complete with religious symbolism. Take the Holy Ghost Horse, for instance. The Holy Ghost is a betting tool brought into play when a certain number has come up a winner twice during the day and you bet it to appear a third time. You go for the trinity.

Then there's the "South American" betting system, where you

look for a jockey who's already won two races on the day to win a third. Riding two winners is a good day but winning three is good publicity. That's called an "Ecuador," and I have no idea why.

A LAFE BASSETT

guy at Santa Anita named Bodie Smith had a sure-fire system. He used to be a clocker and a timer, and after he retired he still came out to the track every day. He'd get four separate programs and stick them in four separate pockets of his sport-coat. On the first program he'd circle the favorite in each race; on the second program he'd circle the second favorite; on the third, the third favorite; and on the fourth, the fourth favorite. And he'd sit there and watch the races, and when the third favorite, say, won, whatever guy he was standing next to, he'd tell him, "Shit, I had that marked!" And he'd go into the appropriate pocket and pull out that program, and show the guy that it was marked. And that guy would think, "Hey, this fella knows what he's talkin' about." If it was the fourth favorite that won, why of course Bodie would pull that program, and so on. He always got two or three guys out there who'd think he was a genius because he'd just keep showin' 'em how he had the winners circled for each race. He'd hustle three guys, and in the next race he'd give one the favorite, one the second favorite, another the third, and so forth. He got several different bets going in every race. They'd pay him for his tips, but it was just a matter of time before he'd burn them out.

So much of it is just dumb luck. I mean, it's easy to out-smart yourself. One time I meet this guy, a big, huge football player from San Diego. The guy's got to weigh three hundred pounds, just enormous, well over six feet tall. I'm five foot five, so he looks absolutely gigantic to me. Anyway, he comes out to the Del Mar racetrack, and he don't know a pony from a starting gate. He asks me who I like in a race and I tell him, "Well, this gray horse that's been training off the grounds doesn't even have a stall here and just comes in to work. This horse looks like he can run pretty good, I'm going to bet him." So, the big guy says okay, we go and bet the horse, and meanwhile I'm explaining to the guy what's going on. The horses leave the gate, and this colt gets left; he's caught behind a wall of horses, but as they turn for home here he comes, flying on the rail, the rail opens up and he runs second. The big guy is thrilled because he bet the horse to place and show and he went off at eight to one, so he wins about two hundred dollars. I say to him, "Boy, this colt is running real good; I'm sure going to bet him the next time he runs." The big guy says, "Oh yeah, I am, too," and he writes down the horse's name.

About ten days later I pick up the *Form*, and I see that this colt is entered in the Del Mar Futurity, going into a stakes race for all winners. Well, this colt had never broken his maiden. I can't imagine why they've decided to enter him in such a tough spot. I figure, you gotta be kidding me, I ain't going to bet a dime on him in this race. Just before the race goes off this big football player grabs me. I'd forgotten all about him, but he's all excited and pounding me on the back. "Hey, Lafe," he says, "I been lookin' all over for you. I took that two hundred dollars I made on that colt the other day and bet it all to win on him in the race today. I bet it all the way." So I think, "Oh shit, this guy is goin' to kill me." The race goes off and the horse wins. He wins! Pays $104 to win! This big guy wins a shitload. He just grabs me and shakes me and shouts, "You're a freakin' genius, man, a genius!" Man, you're right. Thanks a lot, pal. I ain't gonna tell him I didn't bet on this horse. "How do you do it?" he shouts. "A hundred and four dollars to win! You're the greatest!" Yeah, that's me, the greatest. I couldn't believe it.

HOLE-IN-THE-WALL LOUIE
PROFESSIONAL TOUT

You'll love this one. The other mornin' I'm down in Max Milano's barn and he shows me a horse that's going to run that day, that he's the substitute trainer for; he's runnin' him for another guy that owns and trains him. He tells me, "Look at this horse, this horse shouldn't be runnin', but the guy owns him's gonna run him. This horse has a broken knee." The vet is there, he's pushin' on the horse's knee. He says, "This horse is lame, this horse should never be runnin' today." But the owner insists, so they're runnin' him.

Okay. So I go upstairs, I see an associate, and I'm lookin' at the program and see that this horse, Crazy As Hell, is listed as ten to one in the morning line in the fifth race. This associate comes over to me and says, "Hey, Louie, I got a horse for you in the fifth race."

I look at him and say, "Not Crazy As Hell, right?" He says, "Yeah, that's the one." Goes on about how this horse has dropped into the right spot and he can win this race. I said, "Hold on. I just saw Max Milano and the vet down in Max's barn and they said this horse should be shot. It has a broken knee and shouldn't be runnin'." So all right, I tout him off the horse. I got some other business to attend to that afternoon, so I leave the track before the fifth race.

That night I'm walkin' into my house and the telephone rings. It's my associate. He says, "In case you ain't already heard, I just wanna be the first to tell ya that Crazy As Hell won the fifth race, and handily. I didn't bet him." And he hangs up.

The next morning I get down to Max's barn real early and I ask him what the fuck happened. Max says, "It just goes to show ya that you never know when a horse is gonna run, right? Doesn't that just blow your mind? Not only did the horse win the race," Max tells me, "but I bet on him!" "Whaddaya mean?" I yell. "How could you bet on a horse with a broken knee?" "Well," he says, "I got down there in the paddock with him and all of a sudden he starts prancin' around. I know that the horses he's runnin' against are worth a total of about eighteen cents, and I'm standin' there watchin' this horse and he's pawin' the ground, prancin', hittin' on all points. I just *knew* this horse was gonna win," he says. "His adrenalin was flowin' and bam, he was a racehorse! So I ran to the window and got down on him. The boy takes him around, and he wins easy, no problem at all. The horse is lame comin' to the paddock, but he runs like a tornado once he gets on the track. You wouldn'ta believed it." "Right," I say, "I wouldn'ta."

Max tells me that after the race the horse looks the same as he did before, limpin' around. And the next mornin' he's not even standin' on that leg; he's a three-legged horse standin' in his stall. It just goes to show ya that sometimes what ya don't know won't hurt ya. I call this story "Bury My Heart At Wounded Knee."

BUDDY ELDORADO
PROFESSIONAL HANDICAPPER

I was fourteen, in my first year of high school, I cut classes with some kids and they said, "Let's go to the racetrack." So we went. This was in 1947. I thought it was a neat idea to go out to the racetrack because I'd never been there before. When we walked in the first thing I noticed was the odor of horse manure, and it just did not impress me at all. In fact, it repulsed me. Some of the people I went with were older than I was, or at least they looked older, so they could go up to the windows and bet. I didn't understand what they were doing, so I asked questions and found out that they were actually betting on these horses. I mean, I really had no idea what was going on. The one thing that did impress me, however, was that there was a lot of money changing hands. When I looked at the pari-mutuel windows it looked like a bank. You just had to figure out how to make a withdrawal.

So I kept coming back and observing the scene. After about a week, I began buying the *Racing Form,* just to see what it was all about. I started buying the *Form* on a daily basis and hiding them because I didn't want my folks to find out. I saw, gee, there's all kinds of numbers here, so there must be some way to be able to take these numbers and do something with them if I'm going to go and bet. I have to know something about the game.

Well, about six months went by, and I went back to the track a few times, not betting. I hadn't made a bet. I kept reading and studying the *Form,* and I noticed that there were patterns that would come up over and over again. And I thought, "Well, is there any way this could be used to go to the track and make a wager and come out ahead?" I found that if I broke it down into five different categories, separated the statistics in a particular way, that I was able to make a little bit of money; not a lot, but a little bit. And then one thing led to another.

The five categories that I figured out at that time were based on horses that showed a certain pattern. I went back and looked at the winners in claiming races, and found that there were three distinct areas in the claiming ranks. I separated them into a low class, a middle class and a high class; and by seeing the way the horse finished, the amount of weight it carried, the amount of money it ran for, a combination of things, I could get an indication of what the horse would do in the next race. This worked out fairly well for me. I was able to hit approximately one out of three horses that I could win on a consistent basis.

But then I discovered that there were other things involved. The longer I went, the more time that I spent at this, the more I realized that it could become even more scientific, that I had to refine my research. About fifteen years ago I started working with a computer, and I hired a programmer to come in and take my ideas and write a program for the computer so that I would be able to input the information myself. Well, it turned out to be a giant fiasco. I paid the man ten thousand dollars and got absolutely nothing out of it. It was just completely unworkable, mainly because I didn't know anything about programming and this gentleman did, and he didn't know anything about handicapping. So I was at his mercy when we tried to make the program work, and it just absolutely bombed. I finally got rid of the guy and bought a computer myself, a small one, and learned how to do my own programming.

My feeling is that watching the horses run is boring. It has to be one of the most boring occupations I can imagine. I don't see how anyone could sit out there at the track day in and day out unless they're making money. If they tell me that it's fun and relaxing, I can think of a hundred things that I would rather do than be there at the racetrack if I wasn't making money. I consider the racetrack my place of business. I derive my income from the track. I am an investor. If I am investing my time, then I expect to make a return on it. Very early on I felt that it had the potential to become a very lucrative business for me.

I bought everything that was ever written about handicapping, any type of system, and what I found out was that these people who wrote these books were actually not making money at the track.

They were selling systems, and that's how they made their money. That's how they supported their gambling habit. If you use any of their systems, that's what you're doing. You are not making money, you are gambling, and I do not gamble. I hate gambling.

My definition of gambling is when you put money out on anything and you have no idea what your expected return is going to be. You must know what your expected return is going to be, then you're not gambling, you're investing. If I play ten races, I could lose all ten. I could play forty, and I might lose forty. But if I play a thousand, or ten thousand races, I will win fifty-five percent of them. I can guarantee that I will win five out of nine on average, betting only to win, and there is no way you can go broke doing that. So I don't consider it gambling.

When I began doing it I was not that sophisticated, of course. But I was still able to make money on a consistent basis. Anyone that can win one out of three races will make money, but they will have to limit themselves to the odds that the horse pays, whereas now my break-even is approximately even money or just under even money. At first, when I was winning one out of three races, the horses would have to be getting two to one at the very least; I could not bet on anything less than two to one or five to two in order to make any kind of money.

If I win five out of nine races on average, my return on investment capital is greater than 150 percent. In other words, for every dollar that I bet I get a return of two dollars and fifty cents. Therefore, you can sit down and figure that my actual break-even, where I would have what would be termed an underlay, would be odds that were less than even money. Anything over even money that I bet is an overlay to me. Now, I have talked to other people who profess to be handicappers, and I have nothing to go on except for their word. I haven't seen anything. I don't desire to know anything. I try to keep away from most of these people because in my estimation they're a bad influence. With me it's strictly business. I'm there for one thing, and that is to show a return on my investment. If I can't show a return on my investment, then I have no desire to be at the racetrack or making a bet on any type of wagering system that pertains to horses.

What I have is not a system. It's actual handicapping, and by that I mean I'm using statistical analysis, laws of probability and laws of average. Everything in this world depends on the laws of physics, and there are certain laws in physics that say that everything is unknown. I can give an example: If you take a penny and flip it, that penny has a fifty percent chance of coming up heads or tails. However, nobody sits down and thinks, "What happens if it lands on the edge? What are the probabilities of that happening?" You don't know. So anything can happen, but if you flip that penny a million times and it comes up heads a million times in a row, you would have a pretty good idea that the next time you flip it it will probably come up heads, because there's something wrong with the penny. That doesn't necessarily mean that's what's going to happen, but if you were going to make a wager you would be stupid to wager against that, even though the so-called probability is a fifty-fifty chance.

There is nothing in this world that is sure. There is only a probability, and when you are making bets, or you're buying property, or you're making a business decision, the only thing that is sure is the amount of work that you've done to see what the probabilities are. Wagering on horses is a business. People talk about money management; people sell systems on money management. If a person was hitting only one winner out of five races and bet only one percent of his actual pool, there's no way his pool would ever go broke. It just won't happen because it's the same thing as drawing two parallel lines, then stepping in the middle and drawing a third line, then taking half of the distance between those two lines and keep on drawing one line after the other one; you'll never reach the second line, even though the space between the lines is getting smaller and smaller and smaller.

When I hear people say they went to the racetrack and lost their operating capital, it's pretty obvious to me that they didn't know what their percentage of return was going into the game; and they did not know what the optimum percentage of their pool was; and they didn't know what their actual return on investment was. You have to know this before you go into any type of game where you are playing with odds, whether it be horses or dogs or anything else.

Making a flat bet means betting the same amount of money on each bet. This is basically what I do. However, I bet four percent of my operating capital. If I have a hundred dollars in operating capital to start with, for example—it could be any amount—I bet four percent of that hundred dollars, which would equal four dollars, until one of two things happen. Either my pool increases, and I go over a hundred dollars; or I only have forty percent of my pool left, forty dollars. And then at that time my bet becomes four percent of whatever's left over, which would mean at that point that I would only be betting two dollars on a race until I went broke. To give an example: I had a streak once of twenty-nine consecutive losers, the longest I've ever had. The funny thing is, all of those twenty-nine horses finished second. I then proceeded to have thirty-nine winners in a row. I've never had that streak again, either. I once had thirty-eight in a row and thought I was going to break it, but I did not.

I never bet a horse to place, to finish second, unless I am betting only one horse in the race and the odds on that horse exceed forty to one. Then I might bet it to place in addition to betting it to win. Anybody who knows anything about betting at the racetrack knows that if you look at the mutuel pools you'll see that fifty-eight percent of all the money goes into the win pool; the rest goes into the place and show pools. The problem with place and show is what's called breakage, which means that they only pay you to the nearest dime. This is called dime breakage; they used to have nickel breakage. That will account for as much as four percent. Now four percent does not sound like a lot, but if you're betting a million dollars a year that turns out to be forty thousand dollars. I know people who bet considerably more than a million dollars in one year, and that's why I do not bet anything except to win. And when you win five out of nine races, why would you want to be betting place? I mean, it makes absolutely no sense from a business standpoint. Sure, I've had many races that were very close, were what I call a woulda-coulda-shoulda. I might have made money on that race, but over the long haul you will make twice as much money betting win as you will to bet place, no matter how good you are. If you hit one out of three to win, you'll hit approximately forty-five to forty-eight percent to place, and you'll break even or you may make a few dollars. If you hit five out of nine, you might hit as high as seventy-five percent to place, but your payoffs aren't as high.

Actually, what you're doing is if you were going to the bank and they've got two types of accounts, one in which they pay you seven percent and another they pay you ten, why would you put your money in the seven percent account? And that is one of the things that I do not understand about people who go to the racetracks and profess to make their living at it, why they bet to place or show unless they're betting, say, a parlay, a show parlay. I could see where you could take twenty dollars and that's your total invest-ment for the day, and continue to bet show until your minimum bet was up to two hundred dollars a race, then just bet two hundred dollars to show. You can do it that way; I've done it. Not to make money but just to prove that it could be done. But as a steady practice it's ridiculous. Why should you do that?

There are three types of gamblers: The recreational gamblers, who comprise perhaps ninety percent of the people who go to the track, go with the idea that they can afford to lose a certain amount of money, they have already programmed themselves to be losers. The second group, who comprise approximately eight percent, are the compulsive gamblers, people who don't necessarily have to be at the racetrack, just at any venue where there is gambling, any casino; and these people are easy to spot, they're highly emotional as a rule. The third type are there for one thing and one thing only: They're business persons, at the racetrack to invest; and this is the category to which I belong. I know how much I'm going to make, I know what my return on investment capital is. It's akin to the people who go into commodity trading or the stock market. Two to five percent are successful. I would venture the guess that perhaps two percent of bettors at the racetrack, the ones who go virtually every day, actually make a living at it. I am one of those.

My research has shown that fewer than five percent of the races cannot be played. Most "smart" horseplayers are content to lay off races, to wait until they have what they feel is the right situation to bet. And they're right to do that, of course, because that's how they operate. But the only races I have to stay off of are the type wherein there are so many first-time starters that I cannot get a proper line on the race. In order to bet those races you must know something about the breeding, the pedigree of the horses, the trainers, the owners, the jockeys, and I don't worry or know about any of them. I never take into consideration *anything* but the numbers. *Nothing* else. When I see the owner, trainer or jockey carry the horse across the finish line, then I'll start paying attention to anything other than the horse.

Here's an example. In 1975 there was a race that resulted in the biggest single payoff in California stakes history. Approximately fifty percent of the total pool was to win and place. The horse paid over two hundred dollars to win and something like seventy dollars to place. The owner and trainer were interviewed after the race and were asked how much money they'd bet on the horse. They answered honestly, I believe, and said that they hadn't even bet two dollars on him. They did not expect the horse to win. Well, I had this horse along with my key horse; it was one of those few races where I bet two horses. I won somewhere in the neighborhood of forty thousand dollars on one race. So much for taking into consideration anyone but the horse.

Had the owner or trainer known what pattern to look for, the horse would never have gone off at more than fifteen to one. Most pricemakers, you know, will not automatically lay a horse more than fifty to one in the morning line because they want to make it appear feasible to *someone* that the horse just might come in. Usually horses are not made, say, ninety-nine to one, even though they might deserve to be, unless the pricemaker assumes the horse will be scratched prior to race time. It's also considered impolite to the owner and trainer of that horse. If he lays the horse at fifty to one, that's enough of an indication that the horse has no chance in his estimation, and the crowd will usually take it up to a hundred to one or more. If that horse happens to conform to a winning pattern, I bet on it anyway, and it's better for me. I pay attention only to the numbers. I rule out the so-called "human element."

A woman trainer a year or two ago had a horse that came in and paid eighty-some dollars to win. After the race she said she didn't bet on her horses. She said she made her living training horses and winning the purse, and she was satisfied doing that, and I respect her for it. She's a person who knows what she wants to do and does it. I don't know any owners or trainers. I've done very well without them, on my own. My feeling is that if I don't make the selection myself, even if the horse came up to me and told me he's going to win, I will not play it. It can be difficult sometimes but I stick with my statistics. The other day there was a horse that I just knew would win, but my statistics told me to bet on another animal. My horse finished third, and the other horse won. This was not the first time this has happened, but I have seen too many times the thing turn around and my horse will come in, pay twelve to thirty-five dollars, and the public favorite will finish up the track. I must bet the proven way, the way that makes money. That's my sole criterion.

This is what I base my investment on—there are several things that I look at, three basic factors that I have found mean anything at all in handicapping: an analysis of speed; the relationship of each horse to all the other horses entered in the race (the class of the horse); the consistency of the horse. However, the way I approach this is not like an ordinary handicapper. I have discovered formulas that I have worked out by which I can incorporate factors regarding horses coming from other tracks. I don't worry about whether a horse has been off a very long time because I have a way to take care of that. It's very, very seldom that I will not come up with the right horse if it's been off. I use a computer because it helps speed up my handicapping. It gives me a printout sheet so that I have a constant reference. I used to keep all of my charts going back to 1947, but I don't any longer. I just don't bother. In fact, I get rid of old *Racing Form*s and everything. I may keep a data base for three months, five years on *Racing Form*s. I keep a log of purse value, so that I know what the competition is. In addition to that I keep a log of age groupings and sex groupings. I know how to read the race conditions. I probably know as much or more than anybody in the country about race conditions. I study these. I probably could write a book on it, but I'm just not interested in doing that. I use it for my own business.

I would say that anybody who is going into racing, into investing in the racetrack, has to take two or three years of back issues of the *Daily Racing Form* and go through each of them and mark out all the winners. The patterns are there, they're clear. Anybody can do what I am doing if they have the fortitude and mental discipline. I know a man who lost over three million dollars at the racetrack, a compulsive gambler. He gambled away businesses, he went through two divorces. He attended meetings of Gamblers Anonymous. He just could not get away from it. Now this man could out-handicap me blindfolded and with both hands tied behind his back. He lacked only one thing, he had a fatal flaw: The Ironman got him. That's my name for the tote board, The Ironman. This guy would have the greatest selection in the world, a mortal lock, if you will; a horse that could not lose. But if the horse was not paying four to one or less he wouldn't bet on it; he'd bet on something else. And the horse he'd originally selected would come in time after time after time. He literally wanted to punish himself, and he did a very good job of it. The Ironman got this guy in his grip, and the guy could not shake loose. It was a tragedy.

You have to have the mental fortitude, the discipline, because that's what this business demands: discipline. When you go to the racetrack you don't go with friends or relatives; you don't drink; you don't smoke; you don't eat. When you arrive, you've already

made your selections; the only time you'll have a change in selection is if a horse is scratched, removed from the race for some
reason at a late moment. If it's scratched in the gate, you get your
money back and go on to the next race. That's the way you have
to approach this business. I don't know of any other way to do it.
Now I'm sure there are people who are very successful who would
look at what I do and say, "Oh, hell, that's too much work." But
I don't know any other way to do it.

As I've said, I have bought probably every system that's come
out—mainly just to catalog them and put them in my library. This
includes computer programs. And like I say, these people are just
basically selling the program. My feeling is that if someone came
to me and said he'd give me a hundred thousand dollars, a million,
for my system, I wouldn't even consider it. If someone gave me
ten million, why should I? Because I am playing against the sum
total of all the people there at the racetrack. Why should I share
my knowledge? Why, if I can go out there and approximately once
in every two hundred-fifty bets hit a horse that pays in excess of
eighty dollars, should I tell people what I'm betting on? I mean,
that's stupid. If I know what I'm doing, I'm not going to sell it at
any price because it's a living that I can make until the day I die
even if I go deaf or blind or anything else. I can continue what I'm
doing.

There are people who make their living off the horses, people
like me who actually go out and bet them, put their hard-earned
dollars on the line, back their opinion with hard cash. Then there
are those who sell information. If you know or have a pretty good
idea of which horse is going to win, why on earth would you sell
your information for a dollar or two dollars or five or fifty or a
hundred? You could go out and take that same amount of money
and bet it on the horse! Keep your mouth shut, and make fifteen
to twenty times that amount. What these people who sell information are doing baffles me, unless it's just to support their own
gambling habit. I see no other reason to do it. Either that or their
information isn't very good, and they'll lose customers quickly if

that's the case. Of course, new people come to the racetrack every day, and the guys selling tout sheets will always have new people buying their picks. There really are only a handful of people who come to the racetrack every day. There used to be more.

Since the great majority of racetrack patrons are recreational gamblers who don't really have any information other than what's picked in the newspapers or what's picked on the cards sold at the track, you can see the advantage the racetrack has. Now the people who put together these cards and who are paid to make selections in the newspapers are really pretty good handicappers. They have to be or they won't stay in business. But I think what happens to them is tantamount to what happens to the guy who buys a bar and becomes his own best customer. I have never bought a tout sheet because I feel if I can't make the selection myself, I won't bet. It's very easy for me because I don't like gambling. I've actually been thrown out of casinos for not playing. I'll sit down in one and watch the people, but unless I know precisely what the odds are and that I can win consistently, there's no thrill in it at all for me. The only other game that I can see that you could make a predictable profit on is poker, card games, where it's a matter of percentage, a game of skill.

The people who write books about betting just do not interest me. Tom Ainslie, whom many consider to be the father of handicapping, has probably written a dozen books on handicapping. I would be surprised if he's ever made a bet in his life. And I don't mean to be disrespectful when I say that. If you follow what he says, you might be successful over the long haul; he may be right. He gives you the facts and figures, tells you how he plays the horses; but then conveniently at the back of the book he gives you one hundred systems. Now my feeling is, why would you do that? If you've got even *one* system that works, why give ninety-nine others?

There are as many ways to handicap horses as there are horses multiplied by the number of handicappers. I have never, even though I have the money, walked out to the track on opening day and started with a $500-a-race bet. No way. Each year that I've been doing this I take a small amount of money and build it up.

To me, there's a hell of a lot more gratification in taking a small amount of capital and watching that sucker build up than there is to walk out there with $12,000 or $15,000 to start with. That's easy; virtually anybody can do that. What I like to see are the books and programs by fellows such as Andrew Beyer and William Quirin, the experts. And don't get me wrong, these guys *are* experts. These people serve a purpose. Whether they're teaching the correct thing, I can't say. But for my purposes, speaking purely for myself, what they teach me is very important. And that is, whatever they say, do the exact opposite. That's a very valuable piece of information as far as I'm concerned. You need that. You cannot develop a pattern of success unless you know who the losers are. Once you know who the losers are, once you discern properly the pattern they are using, if you do everything but what they do you will probably be successful. This is basically what I've done in handicapping.

I look to find out what the person's credit is. There's a man I know who advertises in the *Racing Form* who has won a couple of handicapping contests. And people who know what I do have suggested to me that I enter one of these contests. I don't go into them for the following reason: These contests are set up over a three-day period, for twenty-seven or thirty races. There is so much luck involved in that that I would be taking my money and throwing it away. I'd be better off going to the track and making my regular bet. People say, "If you win five out of nine races that means you're going to win fifteen out of twenty-seven." But that's not how it works. I could lose all twenty-seven. That's gambling. I've spoken with people who run such contests, who have asked me if I'd like to come in and be part of it. I tell them no, not the way the rules are. I would do it if we played five hundred races, winner take all. Then I'll enter. Or a thousand races, or five thousand. That would be even better, because I know that as the numbers are bigger, as the statistics climb, the more accurate I'm going to be. Another problem with the handicapping contests is that the racetracks want to use your name for publicity, and that's not what I'm after. I've got the fortune, I don't require the fame.

If I was not making money, you wouldn't catch me near a

racetrack. My feeling is that if you've seen one race you've seen them all. You don't have to watch races to win money. A recent fad, a way for more people to write books on handicapping, is what they call "trip" handicapping. This means that they get a detailed account of the horse and its start from the very beginning of the race to the end. I have heard countless people who call themselves professional handicappers say my horse got pinched off, or he got this, got that, lugged in, lugged out, tripped, fell, hopped in the air, ran wide, did all of these things. My only answer to this is, how can I win at least five out of nine races and I've never looked to see where the horse was or what he was doing or what was happening to him? I've never looked to see if a horse was sweaty, whether he was wearing bandages or anything else. Blinkers, shadow rolls, and so on. How can I do that? It might seem impossible but it's the truth. I've been ignoring all that for years. The only thing I attribute it to is that I'm working at the numbers, and numbers don't wear blinkers or front wraps.

One exception to this rule is that if there is an off track, a muddy, sloppy track. If my selection is running a route race, a longer distance around two turns, a mile, say, and he's not wearing mud calks, shoes that are put on the horse to give it better traction, then I won't play the horse. The horse has to be able to get a grip on the racetrack. Some horses have a conformation in the hoof that hampers them on an off track. Generally what I've found is that trainers who are running horses around one turn or in a sprint race might not use these special shoes. If they're running around two turns, it's highly unlikely unless, say, a sudden rainstorm comes up and they weren't prepared for it, they would even run the horse. They would try to scratch the horse because they don't want to take a chance on injuring or abusing an expensive piece of horseflesh.

There was a big stakes race about ten years ago in which I graded a horse at the top because he was the only one wearing mud calks. The race was going around two turns so I bet this horse and he paid almost a hundred dollars to win. Afterward everyone was trying to figure out why that horse won, and the reason was that it got a firm bite on the track. The trainer was prepared because he figured that it would be an off track, and he caught the other trainers asleep at the wheel. If this one horse had not been wearing mud calks, I would have passed on the race, not bet it. It would have been one of the few times I would have passed on a race. If it had been a sprint race, I wouldn't have cared, it would not have mattered. I've had horses win by ten lengths without calks on an off track, but they were sprint races.

I've bet at virtually every major racetrack in the United States and Mexico. I avoid off-track betting parlors because they don't pay the same as the racetrack. There's a four percent differential and, as I've said, if you bet a million dollars a year that's $40,000 you'll be out, and I'm not about to pay that. I can hire a limousine to take me back and forth to the racetrack. And the problem with betting races at the casinos is that they limit the payoffs. Some will pay track odds up to fifteen to one. Some will pay up to twenty to one, or even thirty to one. The problem is the size of the bet. If you start betting a fairly large amount and winning with any consistency, they don't want to touch you with a ten-foot pole.

If I ran the casino, I'd do what I call "comeback betting." I would take your bet, no matter how large it was, and lay it off at the racetrack. Then the odds go down. The casinos are in business for one thing, just like me. If you're any good as a cardplayer, if you're counting cards, the casino will ask you to leave. They're in business to take the poor chump who's not there to really make money, who's there to get a thrill or impress his girlfriend. This is a science that I'm involved in. The casinos don't want scientists in there.

I have eleven typewritten pages that I use as a guide when I'm handicapping. I keep ready to hand records of the first level of competition at every track in North America, though I still have those going back to 1947. I must know the level of competition when I'm looking at a specific horse. I need to know purse, especially, because you can tell the conditions of the race that way, and that's of absolute importance when you bet. You can have a horse that looks great on paper, past performance lines and age groupings notwithstanding, but if he has had no competition against the class of horses that the majority of the contestants in the race have had, then you can almost with impunity throw that horse out. Although once in a great while it will jump up and bite you. If the conditions of the race are not in my horse's favor, but the horse is strong in all other respects, I would either pass on the race or go to my second choice.

You see, I can't tell you if I'm going to win the particular race I'm betting on; but I know if I bet enough races I'm going to win five out of nine of them. Not too long ago I had a race that presented a real problem. It was a maiden-claiming race where I had three horses in the race. I couldn't separate them. I could pass the race entirely, or I could bet all three. My statistics said that I had a ninety-four percent chance of winning with one of those horses, so I went ahead and bet all three. As luck would have it, the longest shot of the three came in and paid more than forty dollars. One of the other horses finished second and the other one ran fifth.

What I do is not really strictly a system; rather, it's systematic. If a horse doesn't show this, or that, some information that will put it in contention, then I eliminate it, it's out. Each time I handicap I code each horse so that I can go back to it and look it up and know why I threw it out. I don't know anybody else who handicaps like that. I keep a record of it. I can classify the horse, classify the track, classify anything about the race. A fellow named Pittsburgh Phil once said that anyone who can classify horses can make a fortune at the racetrack. I absolutely agree with him. He is one hundred percent correct. Once you learn how to classify horses, you're no longer handicapping. There's no guesswork because you're working with very, very strong laws of probability and percentages. If you're in business, you're going to do that. You're not gambling any more than if you're opening a grocery store. If you don't have the right location, then you're gambling. If you're consistently and on a predictable basis making money, you're not gambling.

The racetrack works like a brokerage house. Just like Merrill,

Lynch, Pierce, Fenner & Smith. You come in, and you buy your stock. Brokers will tout you on to stocks because they are making their market in it. The salesmen make a commission, of course. At the racetrack they don't care who wins or loses because they automatically take out a certain percentage of the pool. Win, place and show pools pay them about fifteen percent, plus the dime breakage will equal around seventeen and a half percent. On exotic wagering such as exactas, quinielas, perfectas, trifectas, pick six, pick nine, all of this garbage, they're raking in twenty-two to twenty-three percent. Exotic wagering is for amateurs. As good as I am I will not play that stuff; you're just throwing your money away. I did seriously consider investigating exactas, the two top finishers in the race, since they went to two-dollar wagers, because your pool wouldn't have to be as big. But if I can start with a hundred dollars on straight betting, I would have made approximately two thousand dollars to cover the same amount I'd need to bet on the exactas, and my return, believe it or not, is almost the same as I make on straight betting. So why would I want to put up more money?

I have people who know what I do, who understand that I am successful at the game, who come to me and say, "Buddy, I've got ten thousand dollars. Take it out to the track with you and bet it for me." I won't do it, because then I'd be betting against myself. That's why the track doesn't care. They take their cut no matter what. You put a hundred dollars out there and they take out an average of nineteen dollars, and then they take the rest and distribute it among the winners. Plus they have the concessions and Turf Club catering to make money from. They're covered.

I must say that I admire the pricemakers. I couldn't make a line like they do, set up odds on all these horses with so little time and information. Of course, they don't often set up very long odds on horses because they wouldn't get any action on the board. I mean, about eighty-five to eighty-seven percent of all the horses that win are rated at twelve to one or less in the morning line. I'm not rating horses for odds; all I have to know is that my break-even is when the horse is even money. If it's even money or greater, I'm either going to break even or make money; I've got an overlay. That's as far as I go. Coming up with odds is an entirely different business. The pricemaker at a racetrack has to depend on his knowledge of the participants, the owner, trainer, jockey, and do what he can in the small time he's got with speed charts and conditions. He's got to get that sheet off to the printing press in a hurry well in advance of the day of the race. I've got plenty of time to find the one or two horses in the race that I need.

The people who handicap for the *Form* or the track flabbergast me. They amaze me. I wouldn't even know where to start to do what they do, to rank the horses. All I know is that when I get through I have one horse; to rate them in order is a problem I am unprepared for. You see, some of the horses that they would have to rank near the top I eliminate immediately. I'm always on the look-out for a very highly unlikely winner. I know it sounds crazy, but I'm full of admiration for them. They're rating favorites, and the favorites come in under thirty percent of the time, which is not very good, really, if you're betting to make a living. And the average favorite pays around five dollars to five dollars and twenty cents.

It's very difficult for these handicappers to come up with the winners I do. After all, I've gone back and researched literally tens and hundreds of thousands of winners. I've challenged myself to find out what makes a winner. By the *numbers.* And I've broken them down into categories. So yesterday I got beat by a horse that paid twenty-seven dollars. I don't worry about it. I don't look any further, the way I did when I first began. This horse didn't qualify for me because it had been off longer than my cut-off point, thirty-six days; a limit of exactly five weeks. That's about what the cycle is. If the horse is out over five weeks, it must meet a series of criteria that I've set up. The horse had the highest speed rating, the highest of everything, but it didn't qualify because it had not worked more than three furlongs within a specified time. I know by that basis I will lose about one out of forty-seven-and-a-half times; twice out of ninety-five. I'm not going to worry about that. I go on to the next race.

I'm not out there to impress people. Yesterday I won seven, six or seven, of the ten races, including the feature race, which was the second highest payoff of the day. When you get to the point where I am, losing a race cannot bother you. A guy I'd been friends with for almost forty years asked me to show him my winning ticket on a particular race the other day. I'd played a horse that had been off for nine months, had previously had nothing but grass races and was going on the dirt, but had qualified according to my system. The horse won and paid twenty-seven dollars. Well, this guy has been having a lot of personal problems lately, has recently gone through a painful divorce and so on, so when I refused to show him the ticket he got furious at me. He called me a bullshit artist. I simply told him that I had nothing to prove, that I didn't have to show him anything, but that I'd show him how I'd figured the horse. He just raved at me and said I was full of shit. I said, "Well, I'll talk to you later." He said, "Don't bother." What I've found out is that you don't discuss horses with people who are horseplayers because they don't like to hear about people that win consistently. They don't like winners, they want losers.

It's strange but true. Most people would rather you were in the same ball park as the other fifteen thousand people at the track who are losing. "Oh, I lost." That's what they want to hear. You'll always hear about how much they lost; or if they hit a big score they'll jump up and down and scream. That same guy will then lose and go kick the garbage can down the stairs. I can tell so easily if they're a winner or a loser; I can probably tell you how much they've won or lost just by looking at their eyes. I've seen so many of these people, I've studied them.

Now when I go to the track I project what I call my white shield. I am oblivious to anyone around me, any noise. The only thing I tune into is the track announcer in case he has any pertinent information for me. Otherwise, nothing. I mean I'm literally in a trance when I go there. I white light everybody. I've had people say to me walking out after the last race, "You son of a bitch, why didn't you say hello to me? You walked right past me, and I said hello three times!" I don't hear them, and I don't want to hear them. That's why I don't go to the track with people. I will take along a runner, someone to go back and forth to the windows for me; but he knows why he's there, and he's getting paid, so he knows how to behave. And if he doesn't act accordingly I'll find another runner.

Most people who go to the racetrack have what I call The Pump-and-Dump Syndrome. They get pumped up, thinking they can't lose; and then they get dumped when their horse runs out of the money. They go up and down like a yo-yo. They're yellers and screamers. A friend of mine once told me that he could find me at any racetrack in America. I got really worried, and I asked him how in the hell that could be. He said all he'd have to do would be to go out to the infield on the backstretch and look at the stands through binoculars when the horses hit the top of the stretch. "You're the only guy in the stands that will be sitting," he said.

"And you'll probably just be reading the newspaper," he added. I thought he was kidding, but he said, "No, it's that pronounced." So I quit doing that. Now I get up and go to the restroom, or take a walk. I don't want people knowing who I am out there. If they know me, they're going to follow me, or my runner, to the window. They're going to bet on my horse. Or they'll follow me to the parking lot and rob me. It's a very personal business.

I never sit in the same place twice at the racetrack. I used to have box seats but I got rid of them. Too many people were coming around. Too many people knew me, and I just don't like that. I don't know any trainers or owners; nor do I know any handicappers anymore. I am entirely alone out there, an island. In this business you're better off being anonymous, just one of the crowd. I don't bet at the same window. I may be in the Turf Club one day, and downstairs with the low-price spread the next day. You never know where I'll be. Even so there are people I know who run into me, and then they want to talk, ask me who I like in the next race, that kind of thing. I always say that I like them all, all the horses. They want reinforcement, someone to tell them they've made the right choice, and I'm not out there to do that. I'm out there to *take their money*. That's my job.

My definition of a professional bettor is anybody who can show more than a thirty percent return on invested capital on a consistent basis. That means every day. That doesn't mean they're going to win every day, of course. I will have what I call a losing day perhaps one day out of three hundred. This includes my daily expenses, such as buying a Coke, say, my admission fee, my *Racing Form*, the tip I'll give to the usher who shows me to my seat and wipes it off. After all of these expenses. It could be that I'll walk out of the track with ten cents over what I came in with. That's a winning day, too.

I have walked out as a big loser, of course. The most I have ever bet on a single race is $11,000, and I won it. The most I have ever lost on a single race is $9,000 and the humorous thing about that one is that the horse finished dead last; in fact, he almost didn't finish until it was time for the next race! It just didn't play, that's all. My statistics were in orbit that day.

So I don't worry about it. I think about it, but I don't worry. My sweaty palm limit was eleven thousand. I had sweaty palms when I bet that, I'll admit. In that case I had a pool which I had built up to the point where I had got to that particular level of play. I just wanted to see if I had the guts to do it. Now we *are* talking about the human element coming into play. When your palms start getting sweaty, that's a sign. When you have the guts to walk into the racetrack with that much cash in your pocket, considerably more than that, actually, and you start sweating, though you normally do not sweat, and you begin peeling off hundred-dollar bills, one hundred and ten of them, and you see beads of sweat on your palms, you know you've reached your limit. That was mine. Anything above that, I realized, I couldn't handle. I bet the money and I won, but I was dripping wet when I did it. Up to that amount, though, I have no problem.

Maybe if I'd been making that sizable a bet for a year or so it wouldn't bother me. But that's why I start the meet with only between one hundred and five hundred dollars as my pool, because I know with my return on my investment capital that in three to four weeks I can be making anywhere from a three- to a five-hundred-dollar bet with no sweat. And I'm working with money that I made at the track, so my confidence builds. I can begin the season betting at four percent of the five hundred dollars, twenty dollars. If I lose fifteen consecutive races, I'm down to two hundred dollars. At two hundred I'm still only going to bet four percent until I go broke. I could, therefore, go about a hundred races in order to bottom out. Now if I went a hundred races without winning, I'd retire. I would never go near a racetrack again. Realistically speaking, if anyone did exactly what I did, and began the meeting with fifty dollars, excluding expenses, he could play all season on fifty bucks and chances are he'd come out with probably sixty to seventy thousand dollars.

If a person plans on making the major amount of their income from the racetrack, he'll have to do a great deal of preparation. It takes about five years to be really successful on my terms. If someone can do it in less time, I'd like to know their secret. You have to have good mental discipline; your blood pressure should drop while you're at the track, not rise. If your blood pressure goes down when the horses are rounding the turn at the top of the stretch and you're watching this and your horse is running dead last, and you've bet three or four or five hundred dollars on that thing, then I'd say you're probably on your way to becoming a professional.

Or say your horse is leading the pack by fourteen lengths and you've got a thousand dollars on his nose; he's going to pay thirty-five to forty dollars to win, and he gets sixty feet from the finish line and jumps his shadow, goes right over the rail, spooked by the ghost horse. This happened to me at Calder Racetrack in Florida. If you can't laugh at something like that, then you're not going to be a professional. You'll never make it. I was in hysterics, I laughed myself silly. The ghost horse got him, he saw a horse that wasn't there and catapulted off the track. Most people would have been inclined to say to hell with this, and gone home. I made my bets on the others and won the rest of the races that day. You have to know that something like that comprises only one or one-and-a-half percent of racing luck.

You have to have humility in this business. You have to know what the odds are and stick by your figures. You may have to make some adjustments, to work at the game a little harder. You must have a good sense of humor, obviously. You can't get angry if you lose—and you *will* lose. If you're going to have an emotional reaction, then I say, try to smile, because it's a hell of a lot easier to smile than it is to frown. You use fewer muscles, and you feel a hell of a lot better.

Big Steve is one of the shrewdest and boldest handicapper/bettors I've ever known. Unlike Buddy Eldorado, he doesn't use a system per se, but he does have a number of firm beliefs. Big Steve is a man of conviction: he *always* puts his money where his mouth is, and he's not easily intimidated. On a recent trip to Del Mar for the summer racing season, Big Steve and I spent a few days together, during which time I recorded some of his most salient observations and sayings regarding the game. The following is a sampler.

—It's time to beat the favorite.

—Always watch the board because you want to know what the wiseguys are doing. [The professional money that usually hits the tote board late.]

—When all else is equal, play the class.

—The cheaper the race, the less you want to consider betting on the favorite. If it were a better class of horse, it wouldn't be there.

—Weight on a horse means nothing unless the race is a mile or longer.

—Never, *never* buy a tip sheet.

—Bet closers on the turf.

—When you're ahead, bet more.

—Be there at the end.

THE
FUTURE

*"The sport of racing has only one thing to sell, only one appeal
to the public—who has the best horse."*

—*John R. Gaines*

"The Thoroughbred market is just gone. It's really hard to make it."
This statement, made by a Paris, Kentucky, horse-farm owner named
Charles Nichols to a reporter for the Lexington (Ky.) *Herald-Leader*
in February of 1987, might come as a surprise to those whose
knowledge of or interest in horse racing does not extend beyond
the Triple Crown or Breeders' Cup races. The fact is that the
Thoroughbred market is flooded with second- and third-rate stock.

The United States Jockey Club, which has sole responsibility for supervising the Thoroughbred racing industry, estimated that 52,000 foals would be born in 1987, double the total registered a brief fifteen years before.

Central Kentucky, of course, is classic American Thoroughbred horse country, and it isn't only the smaller Fayette and Bourbon county farms, such as Charles Nichols's, that have been put up for sale. The famous Spendthrift Farm, which traditionally has stood dozens of stallions and boarded several hundred mares, has been forced to sell off the major portion of its once mighty 2,000 acres. Add to this the fact that the price of yearlings sold at auction has dropped for three successive years, including a downward average of twenty-four percent at the 1986 Keeneland Summer Yearling Sale, universally considered the highest quality horseflesh put on the market annually. It was at the Kentucky July sale that Robert Sangster of England and Sheik Mohammed ibn Rashid al-Maktoum of Dubai waged bidding wars during the early '80s that brought prices into the double-digit millions. The top price paid at Keeneland's 1987 Summer Selected Yearling Sale was $3.7 million, by Sheik al-Maktoum, for a Northern Dancer colt. Things are definitely in a state of flux throughout the Thoroughbred industry.

Some horse farms are thriving, of course, and the Thoroughbred business seems to be steadily expanding in Florida and California. Stud fees reached their pinnacle in 1984, however, and are expected in most cases to continue to diminish. The overall picture is one of contraction, due not only to overbreeding but an inflationary economy. The Thoroughbred business grew steadily for almost twenty years, from the mid-'60s through the early '80s. People previously uninformed about the industry invested in horse farms and breeding, intrigued by the attendant glamor of racing and the prospect of terrific and speedy profits. During this period an investor could hardly make a mistake. Banks were generous with their funds, believing the business to be beyond the reach of recession. Horse and land investments seemed immune to failure, but in 1986 alone First Security National Bank & Trust Co., Kentucky's largest equine lender, wrote off better than $1.7 million in loans. Land prices in the state may yet to have bottomed out, but the cost of boarding animals and keeping racehorses in training, along with general farm upkeep, continues to rise.

In Kentucky, particularly, depressed farm and oil economies, much of it dependent on Texas oil money that has stopped pouring in, combined with changes in federal tax laws that have worked to the detriment of horse-farm owners, will bring further urban development bound to wreak unwelcome changes on the landscape. For true racing fans, the Bluegrass country *is* horse racing.

Perhaps the most alarming fact of all to those closely connected with the game is the fact that the average age of the racetrack patron is rising. Young people simply are not going to the races. The sport of kings will endure, surely, but in what fashion?

LAFE BASSETT

The greatest horse I ever saw run in my life was John Henry, a gelding that earned more money than any other racehorse in history. To look at him you'd think he wasn't worth fifteen cents. He was ugly, scrawny, but full of heart. If he hooked up with another horse, it didn't matter who it was or if John Henry was sore, overmatched, overweighted. He always gave you a run for your money. John Henry might look like he was dying down the stretch but if a horse came up to pass him, he'd find the strength to push harder. I've seen a million prettier horses, horses considered classier, but none with more heart and determination.

I'm glad John Henry hit the peak that he did because he's probably the last gelding we'll ever see like that. Once a horse shows potential as a three-year-old, he's retired to stud. That's policy in racing now. He'll never get to be eight, nine, ten or more years old like John Henry, like Kelso, and still be running. Once a horse shows how good he is, he's lucky to make it past his third year. John Henry was a marvelous exception in the racing world, though, by any measurement. He looked like a skinny, ugly filly, and his breeding wasn't worth $500, but he was a real champion.

John Henry's all-time money-winning record may be eclipsed, however, because of all the million-dollar races being written now. Horses don't have to run very often in order to pile up earnings due to the increase in purse structures. For example, Alysheba won only one race prior to his victories in the Kentucky Derby and Preakness Stakes in 1987. Had he won the Belmont Stakes, too, not only would he have picked up that purse but the bonus money allocated for a winner of The Triple Crown. Alysheba, as a three-year-old, would have ranked second behind John Henry in lifetime earnings! In only twelve starts, Alysheba would have won more money than Spectacular Bid, Kelso, Affirmed, Secretariat and Buckpasser put together!

MAX "THE PRINCE" MILANO

I see the future as being really great for me as a trainer because there are so many stupid people getting into the business that I feel it has to be an absolute berry patch in about ten years. There's so few people left who know anything that a guy who just stands in the area can't help but make a lot of money due to their incompetence. The young punk gets a trainer's license and a know-nothing owner gets him plenty of horses to wreck. Capital is what'll work. Plenty of capital. Horses are an excellent investment, but if a man can't buy them for himself he's in dangerous waters. The trainer might pick out a couple of really nice horses for the owner and start getting them in shape and tell the owner, "I think we should run eight days from now, there's a good spot for this one." And the owner says, "Well, Mabel and her cousin Irene are coming in from Paducah, and they're not going to be here on Thursday, so we're going to have to run before then." The trainer is therefore forced into running a horse before he's really ready.

What these people don't understand is that racing horses is like an eraser. Every time you take the animal over to the racetrack you take off a little bit, rub a little of him off, shave him down, plane off a little more, and eventually, no matter who you are and no matter what you do to try and prevent it, if you bring him over there enough times, he's going to come back hurt.

I have a filly that we bred this year, and the woman who owns the farm she's at showed me a two-year-old that was for sale. I was really fascinated by the fact that this woman wanted to sell this horse. Well, I would have shot him the day he was born because he's no good as a racehorse and never will be. John Nerud of Tartan Farms, who I believe is an excellent horseman, said that you can only get lucky if you're moving in the right direction. The only way you're going to breed a good horse is from a good horse. John Henry may have sold for a low price but he was a good horse, a horse that always could run, that always had the ability to run. It was just some stupid person who looked at him and didn't understand what he was looking at who thought he wasn't worth much. You have to think for yourself in this business.

The reason we have horse racing today is that two thousand years ago a couple of nuts were lying around in a poppy field and one guy says to the other, "Hey, I think that palomino can outrun this chestnut," and the other guy says, "I'll bet you fifty rubles he can't." And so, two thousand years later, here we are. As far as a horse having the ability to run is concerned, that horse was *born* with the ability to run, and the only one who can take it away from him is a human being. Horses wouldn't have any problems if it weren't for humans.

RICHARD SOMERS

Most tracks don't make much of their revenue from betting on the horses, which is no good. They make most of their revenue off parking lot and food concessions. What they make off of their handle of the betting dollar they have to split with the state. The state just kills the track profit margin, and they offer absolutely nothing to horse racing other than the fact that they allow race-tracks to operate in the state. States in which racing has flourished of late are those progressive enough to have knocked a portion of their take-out down, rather than raised it. They've found that with a lesser take-out they can actually make more money because the dollars turn over more times.

In California, unfortunately, the racetracks' plea has fallen on deaf ears. The state is insistent on maintaining an unreasonable take-out. Even though it's been proven that in the long run they'll make more money by doing it differently, their short-sightedness and greediness persists. It really makes no sense, but that's what's happening. Racetracks need to be upgraded, grandstands need to be rebuilt. Hollywood Park constructed a new grandstand for the first Breeders' Cup races a few years ago, but Santa Anita's grand-stand was built in the 1930s. The racetracks can't afford to build new facilities, and if they are to attract new customers, they have to be improved. The state could certainly supply relief in this area. Racing is in real trouble in New Jersey and in Alabama, it's fighting to combat an unsavory image in general, and the state just makes it tougher.

LAFE BASSETT

In the old days a trainer like Rex Ellsworth would bring great horses like Swaps and Candy Spots to the track, horses that would go on to become champions, but he'd also bring other fine horses, horses that broke down, that didn't make it. I think there were more good horses that could have made it if the proper time had been taken with them. If you got a hold of a Swaps or Candy Spots, you tended not to pay much attention to the other horses. There just weren't as many races in those days and no need to develop the horses that didn't make it right away. There's much more money available in racing today; you've got great horses going at one another all year long.

Owners that pay millions of dollars for a baby start handling him, coddling him, from the beginning. He's got a veterinarian checking him out all the time. He's on a careful feeding program, he gets vitamin shots, blood tests on a regular basis. He gets the maximum attention and effort. Horses in the past had to run bad-legged or half-way broke down. They couldn't scope horses to see if they were bleeding internally. It's like in the *Rocky* movie when Rocky fights the Russian. The Russian in training is hooked up to all kinds of measurement devices, machines monitoring his movements, calculating pressures, registering how hard he's hitting a heavy bag. That's the way a lot of these babies are taken care of now. They take slow-motion films of him running and analyze his performance. If you've got seventeen million dollars invested in a yearling, you'll take advantage of everything available. There's no comparison between what they did then to now.

People are willing to pay more money for one great sire today than they pay for a major-league baseball team! That's astounding to me. They run biopsies on these horses before they decide on breeding. They test tissue samples to find out if they have the correct percentage of muscle fiber before they can run. In the days of Citation and Swaps, Thoroughbreds were broke just like cow horses and put out in a pasture with bulls. The strong ones survived, and the weak ones didn't.

The lower-quality horses, of course, are not treated so royally. Still, the horse is given a clean stall, gets the greatest feed available, is brushed, cleaned up, has a vet checking him all the time, and in turn is asked to run twice a month to entertain us. It's in the trainer's interest to keep the horse running, of course, to keep him profitable, so instead of laying him up for three months due to a little heat in his ankle, the trainer might give the horse a shot of cortisone and keep him going. That happens, sure. You give him the time off if you can afford to do it. In general these animals are well taken care of, they're not bred for slaughter like cattle and sheep and pigs. We don't eat them. You don't name a calf or pig you know is bound to be slaughtered. It's possible that things could be regulated better than they are, but the horses are pretty well kept most of the time. There are probably five hundred races being run on tracks across the country on any one day, so we need the horses. People are paying seventeen million dollars for a baby, forty million for stud syndications. It's in racing's interest for us to keep standards high and the game honest.

TIMOTHY T. CAPPS

EDITOR AND PUBLISHER, *THE THOROUGH-BRED RECORD*

Attracting younger people, getting more people to the track and to other places to bet on what's going on at the track is a question that everybody's trying to deal with right now, and no one seems to have a very clear answer. I think this is a problem that people in other fields, beyond racing, are attempting to deal with as well. It may be that racing is in worse shape than certain other sports in this regard, but perhaps not. There's simply so much out there for people to do, so many activities and so much entertainment to choose from. As leisure time increases and leisure dollars increase they get spread more broadly across a wider base. So how do we get more people, young and old, get a proper mix of population to the racetrack?

My belief is that what tends to attract people is convincing them that we have something of value to offer. For various reasons racing has not done a very good job of publicizing the value it can offer—

the entertainment value or the gambling value. We must understand that gambling is not something that is going to attract every segment of the population. There's a large group of people out there for whom gambling is a nonevent, either from a lack of money or just a lack of enthusiasm for betting on anything. I think we're dealing with a younger generation who by and large have been brought up in a situation where life has consistently been made easier for them, more convenient in most ways. We have to simplify the betting process for these people, improve the ease of the wager. The state lotteries all over the country have made betting easy. The lottery may not be a very good bet, but it's an easy one, a convenient wager. Racing must be able to compete with this in order to attract new people of any age. Convenience is the key to anything, to any marketing of racing now.

There are several tangible ways that we know will make betting on the races more convenient, but they do have the potential to create some problems along the way. Off-track betting, tele-theaters with betting facilities in them and even telephone betting with cable-television simulcast of races are all being utilized to some degree. They've all been successful in one area or another, but these bring about concern in regard to the damage they do to on-track attendance. The question is whether or not this kind of marketing will eventually damage the business and lead to a shrinking industry. How can we get people out to the racetracks themselves? The industry has to come to grips with this situation, and this may cause some pain. We may have to face the fact that certain tracks will close, that fewer horses may be produced; but in the long run we'll generate more dollars for the owners, for the trainers, for everybody in the sport. The use of various technologies, new methods, will get people to bet on the product.

The idea that we can have the best of all possible worlds is probably not very realistic. People know this intuitively, of course, but they don't want to face it and so there is a fair amount of foot-dragging regarding getting into tele-theaters and tele-betting, more off-track betting and so on. People are avoiding the inevitable because of their fear of the downside. Marketing and promotion are clearly important, and that's an area that racing is far behind in. Not all of it is racing's fault, of course; it's only been in the last couple of years that the government has lifted some restrictions on what could be done in terms of advertising gambling. For years there were FCC restrictions on what could be done on radio and television; even now, with restrictions lifted, many radio and television stations are still reluctant to accept the advertising. So there's a barrier there that has to be cracked, and it *is* being cracked.

Racing was just years behind in terms of being willing to go out and sell the product; largely, I think, out of concern over the stigma attached to gambling, and partly out of just a sort of old-fashioned snobbery. The kind of attitude that prevailed was, "This is a great thing, and if people want it they ought to come and get it. We don't feel we ought to go out and advertise and sell ourselves." Now, of course that did not happen across the board. There were a lot of people who did advertise and promote, but too late. Racing got itself into difficulty by falling way behind other sports in this area, and the catch-up process is going to be long and slow and painful. It's going to take many years to have an effect on the population; the benefits will be slow in coming. Most racetracks now have a marketing director and they're trying various promotions, the standard stuff that's done at sporting events like free admissions and cap giveaways. Those things, however, probably have less appeal in racing than they might in baseball or football or some sport where people can readily identify with the athletes, but I do think there is some value in them. It's only been ten years or so since tracks have developed this kind of approach. So while I wouldn't say racing has fallen irretrievably far behind other sports, it's definitely going to be a long, slow process to get the public to reidentify itself with horse racing. My own feeling is that it will probably never do so again to the degree that it was, say, twenty or thirty years ago. I think racing was more popular versus football, basketball or baseball, ratio-wise, years ago, much more so than today.

The thing that has really made the biggest difference for horse racing and other sports, of course, is television. Television has had a positive effect in some cases, negative in others. Racing has not been a good television sport. I'm sure that in the early years this was due partly to the fact that the networks didn't find it particularly appealing because of the gambling aspect. More recently, though, the experiments the networks have made with racing have not proved fruitful from a ratings standpoint. Racing is just not a good TV sport, especially in a technical sense because it's such a short-lived thing. It's difficult to build a half hour or hour program around a two-minute event. For these reasons racing has not gotten much television exposure, and we all know that the sports that have gotten the greatest exposure are the ones that have grown the most, developed the most. This is a problem that's very difficult to overcome, and I really don't think that in the foreseeable future, the next five to ten years, racing has much of a shot at expanding its television market except through the use of local and cable-television programs. Done well at the local level, I do think televised racing will generate new fans. It's a situation where racing's kind of had the door shut in its face by the networks, and so the broad product identification attained by the NFL or college football or basketball or whatever, by having your game spread all over the country by the networks all weekend, is just not going to happen for horse racing. At least not in the immediate future.

A national organization could do much to assist racetracks insofar as promotion is concerned, and there is movement in this direction. The Jockey Club is contributing a quarter of a million dollars, as is The Thoroughbred Racing Association and The Breeders' Cup, to set up a media office. The plan is to establish and use their computer data base, build files, clipping files, and other things, so that they can supply information to the media and others. I think this is something the sport has needed for a very long time. Racing writers and other people have commented that this won't help because it won't expand coverage of racing, and I don't think there's any question that they're right in the short run. In the long run, however, I think it will work. As it gradually becomes embedded in people's brains that there's an 800 telephone number you can call to get certain information, or that you'll be guided to wherever you can obtain the information, as more and more sports editors and people start to use that, combined with the data generated by the office, the press releases and so forth, then I believe it will have its effect. This will take time, but a clearinghouse or storehouse of this kind of information will be of real value. That's actually a project I've been interested in for ten or twelve years; in fact, I wrote a memo on this subject when I worked for The Jockey Club that's probably still in a file somewhere in their offices in New York, suggesting that we do that very thing. The idea got buried for a while but now they're on their way to doing it.

The promotional side of that operation will take a while to develop. They can operate a marketing consulting service that will aid both racetracks and breeding associations; they can coordinate marketing schemes, find new investors, administer seminars around the country and advertise in the *Wall Street Journal* or *Barron's,* offering a day-at-the-races type of event whereby people can be guided through the racetrack or a breeding farm. This would be an educational process, for potential investors, but it's clearly not the fan's side. I don't know what racing can do about reaching the fans in terms of mass national promotions. I don't think The Jockey Club's operation is intended or envisioned as being anything that bold or aggressive. The idea that racing can get together and come up with thirty or forty million a year to throw into television spots and that kind of thing is probably not realistic. That responsibility lies with the local operation, the local racetrack, the local breeding association, to do its own promotional work through the local newspapers and other media outlets. The Jockey Club organization can supply advice and counsel.

Another thing that's been discussed a great deal over the years is having a national standard for racing officials. There is some stirring toward creating an officiating school that would begin by developing examinations for all racetrack officials. If they didn't pass these exams, then they would be required to go through some sort of program until they did pass, and they would also have to take refresher courses and so on. The Jockey Club is involved in this, too. Some of the curriculum and testing has been worked up already, and they're looking for a place to plant it. Among the possible locations are the University of Arizona, which has a race-track management program; and the University of Louisville, which is setting up an equine management program. There have been discussions between The Jockey Club and both of those places about setting up satellite programs for racetrack officials as an attachment to those schools. I think that will happen.

The problem of a lack of universal standards, though, will still remain unless the various state racing commissions endorse the idea across the board. They must agree to certify only those officials who have been to the school or at least passed the exam. The same problem exists in horse racing as in anything else in this country where there is state regulation as opposed to federal; and believe me, I am not favoring federal regulation of racing. A deregulated system has its strengths and weaknesses, and with the state commissions as regulatory bodies for racing they can choose to ignore what the guy next door to 'em is doing, go beyond what anybody else is doing. In order to get a national training and testing system set up, these separate commissions would have to cooperate. Racing officials such as stewards are often politically appointed, of course, and they, in turn, frequently have the ability to hire and fire their own staffs and other officials; in many cases these appointments are also political. So there will be some resistance at state levels to accept a national certification process. Nobody wants to give up their own vested interest. I think it will take a while, but I do believe that eventually it will occur. People will see the sense of it. In order to keep their man in the position, they'll send him to take the course. If about seven or eight key states agreed to it, the issue would be settled. If New York, California, New Jersey, Florida, Kentucky, Illinois, perhaps Louisiana and Ohio, went along, I think the others would fall in line quickly. It's an important program, and I'm very supportive of it.

The Jockey Club conducted a survey last year among fans and found that what they were most concerned about was how legitimate racing really is. People just aren't sure. I think anybody who loses a bet might be cynical about it for a moment, but then it just washes away. I don't think people would come back if they really thought it was that illegitimate. But there are questions in people's minds about what goes on, and if the fans knew that the officials in the stewards' stand and elsewhere have been through some kind of training and testing program and have been reviewed regularly, that would add credibility to the entire process.

The breeding industry was on a virtually uninterrupted bull-market rise for about forty years. Yearling sales statistics and foal crop statistics since the mid-1930s increased on a regular basis. We went back and compared foal crop price increases to yearling price increases, plusing and minusing them, and there weren't many down years. When they were down, they weren't down very much; and when they were up, they usually weren't up all that much. It was just a steady incremental growth from year to year; two percent one year, seven the next, three the following year, with an occasional little dip, and usually those dips occurred right in tune with the national economy. There was a small dip in the late '50s when the country went through a recession; another dip in the early '70s when the same thing happened. Racing was on a pretty good run there for a long time. The commercial side of the business was very stable, exhibiting solid growth. Then, in the mid-'80s, we ran into a wall; maybe even slightly before that in some markets. I think what happened is that we'd gone through a long period of stable growth, and then in about 1976 through about 1983 there was a spectacular jump, a tremendous increase in the growth rate. By any economic standards one wants to employ, that meant that we were being set up for some kind of substantial decline, one that was going to be of very probably historic proportions. So, the numbers got very big, we've gone through a decline, a major one, one that I think could fairly be called a major recession, and where we are now I don't know.

I think we're at the bottom or very close to it. We're sort of treading water, and we may be doing it for a while. I don't know when we'll be able to climb back to the numbers of three or four years ago, but I think we will do it eventually because markets always come around. There's no question it'll take a long time, though. There were certain forces that entered the market in the late '70s that just hadn't been there in that way before. There was an increase in buying from international sources that started off with Robert Sangster and his partners, and they pushed the market up. They escalated it, gave it more visibility. But I think if it had been just them and only them and their partners, along with the Europeans that followed them in, I think what would have resulted would have been a stronger market than had been in place previously, but not one that would have gone up so fast that there would have been such an eventual major decline.

When the Arabs came in, the game changed. They poured in cash in amounts that were just incomprehensible to people. They had it to spend and they spent it, and they continued to spend it. They created new tiers in the market, restructured the market, and in so doing they changed the game a great deal. It splintered the market, and people began to fall into their own levels; it became a different kind of ball game altogether. Buyers got less competitive, basically, because the prices went up until a point was reached where the only players at the top were the Arabs themselves. There were a very few people who could kind of bounce around with them: Allen Paulson, the D. Wayne Lukas group, people like that would pop in. But I think what happened was that a lot of people who had been in the business off and on for years, not necessarily real big players, but a lot of people, kind of got caught looking when the market started to take off. They were mesmerized by the numbers and decided to go with it. It seemed incredible that this was happening, they rocked along with it, and some of them got whipsawed a little bit.

The people who got hurt the most were the ones who came in near the top, the ones who did some speculative buying and because of the price levels were generally forced into depending on bank money. Some of those people got hurt. Each situation is different, of course, and one can make a case for some of the disasters, say that what occurred to various individuals or farms might have happened under any market, whether it be Spendthrift or anybody else; but to me it's just a typical market cycle in any business; we went way, way up in a hurry, and now we've come down. The question is, where do we go from here?

The two things that made the difference in the industry were, first, the Arabs moving in with such enormous amounts of cash, unprecedented amounts of cash, more than any group of people had ever come into this market with; and the other was that when the process got so high so quickly people found themselves having to resort to bank borrowing in ways they had not before. They started using borrowed money, leveraging themselves to a much greater degree than they ever had before. And of course when prices came down the leverage worked the other way. It's that as much as anything else that's the story of Spendthrift Farm. They continued to buy horses and land at the peak of a declining market, and had they not been so overburdened with debt they probably, in the long run, could have made that pay off. The debt burden, however, was tremendous, and a serious problem for them.

For many investors it simply came down to leverage as much as anything. I think people did get mesmerized by the process, and their expectations rose unrealistically. There were people whom I considered to be intelligent human beings who thought, who really *believed,* that we'd never see the end of the rising market, that it would just be self-perpetuating. They deluded themselves. I had a guy say to me, a major breeder, a couple of years ago at Keeneland, that things were going to be very good at the top of the market because people who had come in as buyers at high levels would likewise become sellers and have a vested interest in propping up the market. My thought was that this was phony economics because somebody has to buy those animals, and if you're telling me a guy is going to go in there and sell the horse and then buy it back himself, then we've got no market at all. There has to be a buyer coming in from somewhere. A person may have a vested interest in propping up the prices but he can't prop them up by himself. People were mesmerized by that kind of thinking; the numbers had just gotten so big, and they lost their perspective.

I think what we've seen is a shakeout that's going to be beneficial. One of the things that makes the horse industry unique, and that also makes it difficult to analyze, to forecast, is that unlike so many other businesses it doesn't have any rough economic justice to it. As an example, if I were looking around for a business opportunity, I had some money in the bank, and decided to open up a pizza parlor somewhere, I'd look at locations, study population figures, demographics, traffic patterns, the competition. I'd investigate diligently a whole slew of factors before making a decision whether or not to open that pizza parlor in that particular place. By and large, people do not analyze the horse business that way. They get into it for a variety of reasons and don't seem to worry much about what's out there in the way of competition. They often figure that it's fun and easy to do. It's simple to go buy a horse, so they do it. They don't think it through very well. In the days when prices were going up so consistently, that lack of foresight and planning turned out to be deadly in many cases. It seemed like such an easy game.

Entry to the horse market is so free, restricted only by the amount of money that one has, that it's not like other businesses, especially those where one's living is at stake. If someone puts so many dollars on the line in the pizza parlor, it had better work because you're not there just to watch those pizzas run. I mean, they'd better sell! The fact that the industry is so open-ended when it comes to entry has turned it into a more cyclical business than it once was. It has very long pay-back periods typically, and that creates a problem for anybody who's trying to leverage himself. The leveraging not only hurt people because the market declined quickly if they bought near the top, but it also hurt because of the extended pay-back periods. If you're borrowing short term and your pay-back period turns out to be a long one, then you run into difficulty. I think the old rules of financing, borrowing short to meet short-term needs, borrowing long to meet long-term needs, was not very well applied in the horse industry for a long, long time. The veteran operations, the people with basic common sense, would not borrow long, and that's the secret of their success.

The racing industry is constantly searching for new ways to promote itself. The Breeders' Cup races, for example, are important in this regard, but without necessarily being the wave of the future. It's been a good thing for the sport internally, though I think the jury's still out on what it's accomplished externally. Whether or not The Breeders' Cup will attract more fans for racing is in doubt. We can't predict what will happen, but basically it's been a real shot in the arm. People have suddenly recognized that we can help ourselves, that we can generate cash and pay ourselves purses and redistribute the wealth within the industry. That's been very attractive to people. There have been emulators on a lower scale, and there will continue to be. The Breeders' Cup constitutes a new approach. I like to think it will help bring new fans out but I just don't know. I mean, it's a one-day deal, it's a lot of racing, seven races, and though I'm very much for it, there's a part of me that says four successive hours of televised racing is too much. At the same time, I think it's important to be receptive to the ideas that people have, to try them out, and maybe down the line we'll end up with a shorter program and somewhat different format. It's also possible that the four hours will turn out to be workable. No matter, The Breeders' Cup, as devised by John Gaines, certainly has made the industry feel better about itself, and provided the industry with a new way to look at itself and promote the game. It was a good vehicle to attract investors. But if people were expecting that it would suddenly stimulate the networks and the cable companies to come dashing in, to seize upon racing as a new darling, well, that hasn't happened. I do think that racing will get more television exposure in future years, but I don't see it becoming a major financial breakthrough.

We in racing have spent too much time internally talking about things and feeling sorry for ourselves. I think it's time we woke up and said, "Okay, we can't deal with all of these problems by just complaining about things and waiting for someone else to solve them for us. We have to attack them ourselves, and the net result will be that we'll end up with a sport that's not quite like it used to be." I think that's a real problem for a lot of people. It's a problem for me at some point, but I can overcome my resistance by admitting to myself that it's got to be done. Too many people in the industry are afraid to face a world in which the results are not predictable. It makes a racetrack executive nervous to contemplate the idea that he may be running fewer dates in the future; or, for God's sake, that he may even have to close down. That's a difficult thing.

Intertrack wagering, tele-betting, tele-theaters, convenience gambling—this is the future of racing. There will also come a time when there is widespread legal sports gambling in this country. Racing has an opportunity to position itself so that it will go right along with football, baseball, basketball and other things in a kind of buffet of gambling operations. The racetrack can be at the hub of it all, because racing has one element that the others don't, and that is a long program of sporadic action. Somebody can come to the track and bet on however many races he wants to, while at the same time watch a football game and bet on that, too. What you could have is a casinolike effect with the advantage of having live action as opposed to chips, wheels and cards. This is one of the possibilities that racing has to investigate.

We have to take advantage of the convenience aspect, of what people want in the way of entertainment. We have to understand what we're competing with and attempt to turn it to our advantage, knowing that there will be some casualties along the way. It's an interesting situation to examine. I don't think anybody can predict what the future will be, but it will be better for those in the industry who are willing to analyze the competition and to realize that, whether they like it or not, they've got to make the changes that will benefit them in the long run.

JOHN R. GAINES
OWNER/BREEDER, GAINESWAY FARM*

It was the Spanish philosopher Miguel de Unamuno, I believe, who said that man has always done three things: danced, hunted and raised horses; and I expect those human traits to continue as long as man is on this earth. I'm not much of one to look into the crystal ball and predict what the future of Thoroughbred horse racing will be, but I think man will carry on in his quest to discover who owns the best horse. That's part of our nature and competitive instinct and pride of ownership. Racing is always going to be flourishing throughout the world.

The industry hasn't fallen on hard times; we're just in a fluctuating market. That's the reality of the situation, and there's nothing more to it. I hate to sound simplistic but there are always going to be fluctuating markets. You can't expect any market to double in value every couple of years, including the horse market. The so-called bidding wars at Keeneland didn't hurt or harm racing, either. The purpose of an auction, after all, is to create a bidding war.

I think there'll be a lot more racetracks opening than closing. They'll have to deal with reality, of course, wherever they may be. There are many states left that don't have pari-mutuel wagering. The industry is fundamentally sound and basically healthy. There is so much disposable income available, it *will* be disposed of, and it's up to racing to try to increase their percentage of that disposable income. We should continue to remain in a strong competitive position. Many people are in favor of applying technology to solve all of our problems. They think that somehow technology is going to put everything right. I'm not so sure about that, but I'm sure

*During 1986, the progeny of such Gainesway Farm stallions as Riverman, Lyphard, Vaguely Noble and Apalachee, among others, won or placed more than five hundred times in stakes races worth more than fifty million dollars, resulting in six divisional champions worldwide. Lyphard sired progeny that returned $4,753,169 in earnings in 1986, an all-time season record.

there will be various technological innovations that prove useful for people who bet on the races.

The purpose of racing is to find out who the best horse is, and the purpose of The Breeders' Cup is to focus on that—for different age groups, for dirt and turf. This best represents what racing has to offer the public. The Breeders' Cup doesn't make owners or trainers race horses any more or less; if you've got a good horse, he's going to be raced. Owners and trainers may point them toward different goals than they had before The Breeders' Cup. It's established a racing value system. There aren't too many horses, and there aren't too many races. It's always been the same proportion whether there were two thousand horses racing or forty thousand horses racing. These horses are fragile animals, and they're not really designed to perform these tremendous tasks they're asked to perform. In the normal course of events, horses will break down, there will be injuries, and it's got nothing to do with The Breeders' Cup.

Certain breeders are successful because they operate on the principle that the best producers are the best producers. If you can't start out with the best producers, then you start out with the best performers; and the probability is that the best performers will become the best producers as compared to any other process of selection. How animals inherit is so complex, so complicated, that breeding the best to the best is the simplest way. Why complicate it?

Dosage is bullshit, pure bullshit.

Dosage is a mathematical formula pertaining to breeding that involves blood "dosages"; a system designed to indicate speed and stamina.

Throughout the history of breeding animals, people have come up with all kinds of theories and ideas, and the dosage system is genetically absurd. The problem with all of the dosage systems— Vuillier's, Varola's, the Bruce Lowe Family System—is that there is no control group. Just forget the dosage system. If you take any of these theories and apply them in a negative way, apply them to the horses that finish last on Tuesday or Thursday afternoons at the most meager racetracks around the country, where the poorest horses in the world are struggling for the most minimal purses, you will come up with the same dosage figures as you do for horses who are running for the greatest stakes at the best tracks. You come up with the same figures for the worst as well as the top horses.*

If people don't have a genuine love for the animal, a sincere desire to be involved in racing, they should not get into it, because economics has never worked for anyone at any time in the history of the sport; and it *is* a sport. It cannot be analyzed in typical business terms. You take all of the purse money that's available throughout the world and divide it equally among all the horses in the world and you come up with a number that's incredibly negative. This is basically always going to be true. Unless you're a sportsman and love the game, unless you enjoy the ambience, the world of Thoroughbred racing, don't get into it.

*Note: The dosage method has accurately identified every winner of the Kentucky Derby since 1928.

EPILOGUE

It was the last Sunday in October in Paris, a sunny, cool day, and I accepted my friend Alexandra's invitation to accompany her to the races at Longchamp. Alexandra's family owned several Thoroughbred racehorses, though none were scheduled to run that afternoon; a couple of them, she informed me, would be going later in the week at Maisons-Laffitte. We drove through the Bois de Boulogne and parked in a muddy field beneath a chestnut tree.

I bought a program at the entrance and discovered that we had arrived too late to bet the first race. I noticed that there was a horse entered in the second race named Phoebus. My daughter's name is Phoebe, so as soon as we reached the *propriétaires* section I went to the window and bet one hundred francs to win. As we found our seats the race began. Phoebus stayed in the middle of the pack until the top of the stretch, at which point he broke through on the rail and romped home four lengths in front. He'd gone off at five to one, so I was off to a fine start.

Alexandra introduced me to the people on either side of us. The parties in this section each have private boxes; they all own horses, and know one another well. On our right was a Greek shipping tycoon, a handsome, middle-aged man, with whom I shook hands, and a beautiful young blond woman whose name was not mentioned. On our left was an octogenarian Polish count who resembled the poet Ezra Pound; he nodded slightly and returned his attention to the turf.

In the next race I placed a fairly sizable wager across the board, on a six-to-one shot ridden by the great Yves St. Martin, whom I had seen ride in America. The race was 2,000 meters on the grass, as, of course, all European races are. St. Martin's mount broke on top and stayed there unchallenged until the last quarter of a mile when a big black colt came up at him like thunder. St. Martin's bay stretched himself out, and the jock got his head down at the wire, nipping the black by a nostril.

I jumped up and hugged Alexandra and shouted, "Way to go, Yves!" The Polish count turned and stared at me as if I were a lunatic. The Greek shipping tycoon smiled and his gorgeous blond friend gave me a little wave with her smile. I went off to collect my winnings.

At the cashier's window I was approached by a fellow about my own age, in his mid-thirties, who introduced himself to me as Basran Badran, from Beirut. He was nicely dressed in a blue three-piece suit, and he explained that he was accompanied by his parents, his wife and an uncle, all of whom were seated nearby in the lounge area, sipping champagne and nibbling little ham sandwiches. Basran said that he had noticed my presence twice now at the cashier's window, and he was curious about my betting secrets.

I laughed and asked him if he lived in Paris. "Oh, we come to Paris perhaps once a month," he said, "to do our banking. I used to own several racehorses in Beirut." I asked him if he had any running that afternoon at Longchamp. "No, no," he replied, "and not in Beirut either." "Why is that?" I inquired. Basran smoothed his mustache in both directions before he answered. "A very good reason," he said. "There is no more racetrack in Beirut. It was bombed, as were the stables at which I boarded my horses."

Basran asked me if I owned any of the horses on which I'd been betting, and I explained that I, too, was only a visitor. I told him that I was a writer and asked what business he was in. "My family and I are in commerce," he answered. "Some import, some export." "The war in Lebanon must make things difficult for you," I said. Basran smiled and nodded and caressed his mustache. "War is not necessarily unkind to everyone," he said. "One must be fairly certain, however, to operate within reason. Safe investments, you know, no long shots as at the racetrack. One must maintain one's good habits." He laughed after he said this.

Together we examined the field for the next race, and I told Basran which horse I liked. "A long shot!" he said, and laughed. "This is an American trait, I think, this wagering on long shots. But I will go along with you." I explained that at Longchamp my guess was not quite as educated as it might be at Santa Anita or Belmont Park, but Basran just smiled. "Nevertheless," he said, "I will go along."

Basran stuck with me for two races, both of which we lost. I apologized to him but he shook my hand and told me not to worry, that he had enjoyed making my acquaintance. He would rejoin his family for the remainder of the program. "Remember," he said, "if you are in Beirut to come to see me. But we will have to find an activity of mutual interest other than horse racing." I assured Basran that I would look him up if ever I were in Beirut, wished him *bonne chance* and went over to the ticket window to place a bet.

I placed a modest wager on a filly named Negresse, a nine-to-one shot, and went back to Alexandra's box. She asked me who the fellow was she'd seen talking to me, and I told her. "Did he tell you what business he was in?" she asked. "Commerce," I said.

ABOUT THE AUTHOR

Barry Gifford was born in 1946 in Chicago, Illinois,
and raised there and in Key West and Tampa, Florida.
He is the author of the novels *Landscape with Traveler*, *Port Tropique* and *An Unfortunate Woman;* two
fictional memoirs, *A Good Man To Know* and *The
Neighborhood of Baseball;* a book of essays on film
noir, *The Devil Thumbs a Ride & Other Unforgettable
Films;* and several books of poetry. He is co-author,
with Lawrence Lee, of major biographies of Jack Kerouac and William Saroyan.

Mr. Gifford has been the recipient of The Maxwell
Perkins Award from PEN, a Fellowship in Creative
Writing for Fiction from the National Endowment for
the Arts, a Notable Book Award from the American
Library Association, The Art Directors Club of New
York Merit Award and a PEN Syndicated Fiction
Prize.

He lives with his wife and two children in Northern
California.

"Import and export. He and his family are in Paris visiting their money."

Negresse ran second. I'd bet her across the board, so I made a few francs. I wished Basran had stuck with me for one more race, but I figured he probably didn't need the money. "Your ability to bet on long shots astounds me," Alexandra said. "I could never bring myself to do it. I'm afraid it's just one of those things that can't be taught." "Count your blessings," I told her. The Greek and his lady were gone by the eighth race, and the old Pole was asleep, his wispy beard resting on the handle of his cane.

As we passed out of the gate at the end of the day, Basran Badran and his family crossed our path. "Who did you bet on in the sixth race?" he asked me. "Negresse," I said. "So did I!" shouted Basran. We both laughed and shook hands. "Good luck," I said. "Yes, good luck," he replied, and added, "That is certainly the best habit of all."